"There isn't a kitchen I would rather eavesdrop and peep into than Gabriele and Debi's. *Extra Virgin* has smartly chosen recipes, deft cooking, and drips with easygoing sensuality."
—ANDREW ZIMMERN

"I can't cook to save my life, but reading this book is like walking vicariously into Deb's kitchen wearing her black patent stilettos and screaming in my best Brooklyn accent, 'Get it while it's hot!'"
—MADONNA

"*Extra Virgin* is a soulful cookbook that brings love of food and family together with healthy, light, and luscious Italian dishes. Their book left me wanting more as only food and love can."
—CAT CORA

"The spirit of Tuscany and its delicious, heartwarming, family-oriented cuisine is all over this beautiful cookbook, and will inspire home cooks everywhere."
—NANCY SILVERTON

"This is the definitive Tuscan cookbook, filled with savory recipes, gorgeous photography, and charming anecdotes."
—DREW NIEPORENT

"Recipes made with love by two people truly in love are what you have here. This book is the perfect place to turn for their delicious recipes and love on a plate."
—SUNNY ANDERSON

EXTRA VIRGIN

Recipes and *Love*
from
Our Tuscan Kitchen

EXTRA VIRGIN

Gabriele Corcos

and

Debi Mazar

PHOTOGRAPHS BY ERIC WOLFINGER

Clarkson Potter/Publishers

NEW YORK

Copyright © 2014 by Debi Mazar and Gabriele Corcos
Photographs copyright © 2014 by Eric Wolfinger

Published in the United States by Clarkson Potter/Publishers, an imprint
of the Crown Publishing Group, a division of Random House LLC,
a Penguin Random House Company, New York.
www.crownpublishing.com
www.clarksonpotter.com

CLARKSON POTTER is a trademark and POTTER with colophon is a
registered trademark of Random House LLC.

Library of Congress Cataloging-in-Publication Data
Mazar, Debi.
Extra virgin : recipes & love from our Tuscan kitchen / Debi Mazar and
Gabriele Corcos ; photographs by Eric Wolfinger. — First edition.
    pages cm
Includes index.
1. Cooking, Italian—Tuscan style. I. Corcos, Gabriele. II. Title.
TX723.2.T86M398 2014
641.59455—dc23   2013032506

ISBN 978-0-385-34605-4
eBook ISBN 978-0-385-34606-1

Printed in China

Book and jacket design by Jan Derevjanik
Jacket photography by Eric Wolfinger

All photographs are by Eric Wolfinger with the exception of:
pp. 29, 49, 88, 99, 241 by Jeremiah Alley; pp. 5, 38, 63 by
Lorenzo Carlomagno; and p. 21 by David Lang.
Photographs courtesy of the authors: p. 175 by Chiara Sinatti
and pp. 4, 235, and 256.
Cooking Channel photographs on pp. 8–9, 13, 26, 38, 73,
163, 199, and 231 are provided courtesy of Cooking Channel, LLC.
© 2011 Cooking Channel, LLC.
Cooking Channel photographs on pp. 31, 176, 210–211, and 123 are provided
courtesy of Cooking Channel, LLC. © 2012 Cooking Channel, LLC.

10   9   8   7   6   5   4   3   2   1

First Edition

We dedicate this book to one another,
to our daughters, Evelina and Giulia,
and to families everywhere.

CONTENTS

DA FIRENZE IN AMERICA

A RECIPE FOR LOVE, LIFE, AND FAMILY

DEBI: I grew up with a deep love for food, thanks mostly to a grandmother who cooked well and could win over anybody with her braciole. But it was also because of that truly unique food upbringing that a lot of New Yorkers talk about, where your street could be a meeting place not just for people, but for aromas from seemingly all corners of the earth. There would be fried chicken from one window, spicy island dishes from another, and down the block something garlicky and peppery wafting out of the Italians' houses. And all that might be in the air while I was thinking about the dinner I was about to have in Chinatown!

When I was eight years old, my mother moved us to Saugerties in the Catskills area of upstate New York and essentially became a hippie. She got into gardening—growing corn, zucchini, tomatoes, and basil—and taught herself how to cook, making delicious meals, and baking bread and pies. It was a bit of a culture shock for a young girl with the excitement of city streets in her blood, but it opened my eyes in the best way possible to good, fresh, locally grown food. We had neighbors in Woodstock who were from Northern Italy, and it was at their house that I had my first taste of freshly made pasta, which was always hanging over drying racks and draped over chairs around their

house. Nothing against my grandmother's heavy, delicious Sicilian-style dishes, but this was something special, and different.

I'd always adored Italian cuisine and its well-honed use of ingredients that have been cultivated and enjoyed for centuries. But meeting and falling for Gabriele, I discovered how much great food also comes from a desire to feed the ones you love. I'd always thought I would have to win over a man with my own cooking. I remember plenty of times I'd go to all this trouble to cook for a guy who'd show up late, if at all, and who'd never appreciate the time and effort I put into a meal. At the very least, I had my dinner parties, which had become popular gatherings for my friends. But here was this handsome Florentine, passionate about life, art, history, and food, who not only wanted to cook FOR me, but loved impressing me with the vegetables, fruits, cheeses, and meats of his country, region, and family. Hot, right? Then he took me to his hometown of Fiesole in the hills above Florence, to the beautiful land where his family had lived for generations, and the sense of history was overwhelming. I have a deep fondness for ancient cultures and strong traditions. Gabriele showed me the fruit trees, the wild herbs, and the rustic sweep of it all, and I fell for him all over again.

I'll be honest—merging our refrigerators involved some negotiation at first, mostly when it came to what he thought about some of my food staples. I had good extra virgin olive oil, fresh herbs, quality ingredients for a sauce. But one look at my rice milk, tofu, and bean sprouts, and Gabriele had to control his impulse to take over our kitchen. I would come home exhausted from shooting a TV series, too tired to think about much of anything except learning lines for the next day, and I'd find that my husband had whipped up a dish inspired by his scouring the local farmers' markets. Then I understood what an act of love it is to provide a simple, fresh, and delicious meal for your *amore*. I may have occasionally had my head in the plate, I was so freakin' tired, but you would have seen a smile as my face fell forward!

As our beautiful daughters, Evelina and Giulia, came into the picture, and since Gabriele and I decided to turn our kitchen-inspired happiness into a website to share our joys of traditional Tuscan cooking, our passion for the flavors of my husband's land has only grown. Our

television show has been another outlet for what we're trying to convey. But there's no substitute for this: a book with easy-to-make, joyful meals from our heart and soul.

So please use this book. Dog-ear the pages. Get sauce on it. Let a spray of olive oil from a vigorous drizzle mark its pages. Write your favorite notes—your own inspirations—in the margins. Let the love we put into these recipes become a part of your home. Your family will thank you, the friends you cook for will look at you in a new light, and maybe that special someone you hope to woo will find that decision about you a little easier to make! We crave the spice and sweetness of life after all, and as I've learned from loving Gabriele, delicious food made from great ingredients is the means to achieve it.

GABRIELE: I've walked through olive fields picking fruits of the harvest, and stood by my grandmother as she made ravioli by hand, and stolen a bite of prosciutto from my hidden stash when my kosher Jewish father wasn't home. I grew up with a strong sense of food's connection to the earth, to family, and to personal pleasure.

These are the experiences that make me the Tuscan cook I am today, and I find the greatest joy in life from cooking the food I grew up with for my family and friends. It's the same joy I experienced as a percussionist when I was pursuing a music career—that thrill of performing for audiences. There is a direct connection between doing what I love and the feeling it gives me when I experience it.

It's interesting how often making food for someone else may seem routine on the surface, but inside you teem with deeper emotions connected to caring for others. My earliest memories of learning how to cook come from my mother, a schoolteacher, showing me the ins and outs of the fridge and the stove, so I could make my baby brother Fabio's bottle on Sunday mornings, while Mom slept in after a hard week. (Not waking her up was step one of the recipe.) Feeding my brother was a taste of responsibility and maturity—tied up in providing for someone unable to fend for himself—that I never forgot. Then when Nonna Lola, my beloved grandmother, taught me the secret to her wonderful almond cake, it was like being given a family heirloom, from a doting grandmother to the grandson who cherished her cooking. When I was a newlywed with a pregnant wife, it dawned on me what my life had been leading up to: the ability to feed my family, to turn the making of a fragrant, nourishing bowl of pasta with red sauce into an act of the most sincere love.

When Deborah and I started making home videos to share on the Internet, teaching people the basics of traditional Tuscan recipes, we watched our site grow into a much larger audience. I was surprised at how freeing it was to be in contact with the world through the food I loved. Then again, learning to cook as I grew up was a form of freedom, as was breaking certain rules in our house, too. The funny thing about *mio amore* Deborah's story is that for her, it took leaving the city and landing in the country to round out her appreciation of food. For me, I would often feel stuck on our Florentine farm, longing for the chance to liberate myself from the delicious but restricted palate of kosher eating, which forbids pork as well as mixing meat and dairy. Sure, I learned how to use an open fire to grill steaks, plus guinea fowl, lamb, and pheasant, but I was missing out on the animal at the center of so much Italian cooking:

the pig! I would go to birthday parties and see prosciutto sandwiches and cured pork products everywhere, and then stuff myself like a puppy that doesn't know when to stop eating. There I was, sick from too much mortadella—the delicious cold cut made of high-quality pork, pistachios, and generously marked with cubes of fat—and I couldn't tell my dad!

The recipes collected here represent my deep, abiding love for how Tuscans approach cooking. It's a region devoted to honoring fresh, natural ingredients, using them sparingly but wisely, cooking them with the respect they deserve, and letting their flavors shine. Our food is rustic, but in its own way supremely delicate. It's ideal as a cuisine with which to celebrate family and friends, and through which you can turn yourself into a great home cook. Tuscan food is a language all to itself, and teaching that language as I was taught it by my family is what I hope to do with this book.

I don't believe good food needs to be expensive, or time-consuming. It doesn't even always have to be one hundred percent handmade, especially when more and more grocery stores offer plenty of quality ingredients and prepared items. I know it can be a struggle to stay on a budget, to feel as if there's no time to make dinner, to think you can't make something because it seems too hard. But when you start making our food, you'll feel that much more confident in the kitchen about all aspects of cooking—the shopping, the time it takes, and the techniques—and a lot of those worries will melt away as quickly as freshly grated Parmesan on warm risotto.

I remember the smiles on my own family's faces when I began cooking for them, and that's a goal well worth striving for.

G: Think of your kitchen, pantry, and refrigerator this way: If you had to right now, could you whip up a Spaghetti alla Carbonara (page 74) for a hungry child? Or a Minestrone (page 114) when you're stuck inside the house? Or an Amatriciana pasta (page 69) for an unexpected visit from a friend or relative? We can, because when it comes to shopping, we divide our needs by what's essential and ever present, and what's worth making a special trip.

I know what's in my cupboards and fridge at all times, because for me, shopping is something I look at as perpetual, not a chore to start and finish. Too often in America I see people shopping haphazardly, maybe thinking last minute only about the night ahead, rather than for a rotating menu that allows for variety and invention. I don't go to a store to get inspired. Keep your grocery list on hand!

There's more to shopping than the grocery store, too. Find a local butcher, and get to know what they have to offer. If you have a fishmonger, do the same. They will have the better, higher-grade cuts than your chain supermarket. Become a regular at your local farmers' market. Learning to shop seasonally will automatically make you more conscious about your shopping and what you need in your kitchen.

Remember, the true path to shopping like a Tuscan is thinking about the purity of ingredients, not shortcuts. It's not about flavor-infused olive oil, or prepackaged meals, or a mix in a bag. Once you start making a few of our recipes, you'll start to notice how ingredients go together to best bring out their individual flavors.

So consider our Pantry section (below) a peek into the basics we never like to be without at home. These are the building blocks for a lot of our recipes. You're not going to find specialty items here—meat, fish, that particular cheese, an in-season vegetable or fruit—just the essentials that we believe should be ready to use at all times.

The Pantry

EXTRA VIRGIN OLIVE OIL: This is literally liquid gold for Italians, and should be for you, too. It's a part of nearly every recipe, whether kicking things off in a heated pan, or gracing a dish at the end, or both. This culinary lifeblood is produced everywhere in Italy, but naturally we're biased toward the justifiably coveted, world-famous Tuscan kind, which ranges from pale and effervescent to dark, green, peppery, and intense, depending on the region within the region. What makes olive oil "extra virgin" is how it's extracted from the glorious, dutiful fruit. If the means are strictly mechanical—wheels or rocks or machines that squeeze the juice from the olive without the use of chemical agents—then you have the premium oil, yielding the most fruitiness with the least acidity (below 0.8% to get labeled "extra virgin"). If you've ever seen first cold-pressed olive oil, which is what's produced from a one-time extraction process without using heat, it's so luminescent—green and vibrant—it can actually look like automotive coolant! Our suggestion for what to have on hand is twofold: a high-end, artisanal bottle imported from Tuscany that you use for that final drizzle that anoints your meal, and

a lesser-priced brand of extra virgin olive oil (still Italian, mind you) that acts as your cooking/frying oil. Keep it nice and cool if you can—not refrigerated, just away from too much heat or light—and it'll last a good while.

SALT: When it comes to salting water for pasta, we prefer a coarse grind like **kosher salt**. When finishing a meat or fish, we use either the **granulated** table kind or **sea salt,** which can be coarse or flaky. If seasoning a sauce, we use pinches from a little ramekin filled with granulated salt, because it will melt more quickly in dispersing flavor. It's important to remember that regardless if the salt is fine or coarse, the inherent saltiness doesn't change.

WHOLE BLACK PEPPERCORNS: You always want to grind black pepper as needed. The pre-ground kind loses so much flavor after it leaves the factory that there's no comparison.

HOT RED PEPPER FLAKES: A spicy necessity! We like to make our own flakes by roasting hot peppers grown in the summer, letting them dry for the winter, then opening them up and crushing

them in a mortar and pestle. But there are plenty of good store brands, and we buy those, too.

FRESH HERBS: These are the aromatics that work wonders in all manner of dishes, and fresh—not dried—is the way to go. **Basil** is the sweet herb that gives anything it touches a garden vibrancy, and is the soul of fresh Pesto (page 63). **Rosemary** keeps evil spirits away, if we're thinking like the ancients. It gives such a great fragrant kick to grilled or roasted meat. **Sage** is the essence of wildness and greenness, savory and silky in equal measure. **Bay leaves** bring an almost mysterious depth and character to stews and sauces. And **mint** is simply refreshing and invigorating. Then there's **parsley**, so prevalent as a sprinkled garnish that its Italian translation—*prezzemolo*—is often used to describe people who won't stay out of your business. And yet, there's a tinge of herby cleanliness to freshly chopped Italian parsley that leaving this common adornment out would just feel wrong. You might wonder why we didn't mention oregano, that other ubiquitous seasoning. The honest answer is, we just don't care for it. Buy it if you love it, though!

VINEGARS: We primarily use vinegar in salads. Italians grow up knowing the pungency of **red wine vinegar**, but through Deborah and her love of leafy entrees we've come to appreciate the softer, more delicate, citrus-friendly sensibilities of **white wine** and **champagne vinegars**, and the dark, rich, sweet taste of **balsamic**. An older, especially viscous balsamic is also a great smear on a piece of aged pecorino.

WHOLE PEELED PLUM TOMATOES (PELATI): These are the basis for many of our sauces: sun-ripened, sweet, and full of flavor. We like them whole because it allows us to choose whether we want to purée them, or crush them by hand, depending on the dish. Unless you're in the mood to give yourself extra work during in-season months boiling, cooling, and peeling tomatoes yourself, do what even the big-time chefs do: Enjoy the canned kind, packaged right after ripening, and hardly an inferior substitute. We like imported plum tomatoes from the San Marzano region of Italy (indicated by the DOP seal of approval on the label), but there's plenty of proof that big brands like Hunt's know what they're doing, too. You may prefer to buy 28-ounce cans since they're more economical—just be sure to use any saved, refrigerated tomatoes within a few days after opening the can.

SALAD GREENS: For good old-fashioned crunch, nothing beats **romaine**. Most kids love it. But we are especially fond of **mixed baby greens**, whether **radicchio**, **kale**, **arugula**, or **spinach**. Freshness is of importance to us, so often the type of salad we make is dictated by what our farmers' market has to offer.

ONIONS: When buying onions, look to make sure they're not bruised. Our great fondness is for the **red onion**, which gets used raw when we make Fish Tacos (page 164) or salads, and is most often the basis for pasta sauces because its pungent flavor comes through more deeply. We consider **white** and **yellow onions** interchangeable when making soups and stews. In the end though, if a trip through the produce aisle yields no firm reds, substitute with white or yellow. Firmness is important.

SHALLOTS: We love shallots for risotto and salads—they give the flavor of onion without being as intrusive. As with onions, check for firmness. Even if it looks good on the outside, a quick grab might reveal something squishy and old.

CARROTS AND CELERY: These two vegetables are essential for *soffritto* (page 51). They are a flavor foundation! But they are also delightfully crunchy snacks when raw, especially with a little bowl of olive oil, red wine vinegar, salt, and pepper to dip them in.

GARLIC: You want the most from your garlic, so buying it fresh is key. The head should be tightly enclosed, with no signs that it's germinating or splitting open. You never want to run out of this, so keep plenty of heads available!

LEMONS: We always have these on hand for juicing and zesting. They bring citrusy life to salad dressings, cocktails, vegetables, and fish.

FLOUR: The less-refined **Italian doppio zero flour** is what we use for all our baking: bread, pizza dough, and fresh pasta. It's imported, and therefore more expensive, but you can always use **all-purpose flour** for any of our baking recipes. We always use all-purpose flour for recipes involving dredging or thickening. And if you have an opportunity to buy flour from a local mill, that's great, too.

SUGAR: For every baking need, there's **granulated sugar**. When you need to dust cakes or make meringue, **confectioners' sugar** is essential. We keep **raw sugar** around for sweetening hot drinks like coffee and tea, and for certain cocktails.

HONEY: Don't settle for cheap honey in a plastic bottle shaped like a bear. That dab of high-end sweetness with your sliced cheese is worth the extra cents.

BUTTER: Italians don't like to use salted butter—we're too conscious of our seasoning already. We use **unsalted butter** for most of our cooking and baking.

MILK: Gabriele will drink a glass of cold **whole milk** every day, because he's of the belief that extracting fat from milk goes against how civilization originally nurtured itself. So as you might imagine, the whole kind makes its way into our cooking as well.

EGGS: There's no escaping the difference between yolks from fresh, organic, cage-free eggs and those from chickens grown in cramped quarters, and kept forever in grocery stores. The former have defined layers between the bright yellow yolk and the white, and the latter are pale, soft, and runny.

RICE: When making risotto, we use **Italian short-grain Carnaroli rice**, which has a higher starch content and a firmer texture than the more commonly used Arborio rice. For all other basic rice cooking—as a side with beans, for example—it's simple **long-grain white rice** all the way.

DRIED PASTA: Our pasta chapter dives into this staple in more detail, but we keep plenty (four to six boxes) of dried spaghetti and penne around at any given time.

PARMIGIANO-REGGIANO: It's a cheese—the big cheese, if you will!—but it's so much more. It's as much a seasoning for Italians as salt or pepper. But it has to be Parmigiano-Reggiano, stamped as such on the rind or the packaging, because anything else will have a different saltiness and texture. Don't buy pregrated, either: As it dries, it loses that softness and a lot of the desired flavor. And when you're buying the hunk attached to the rind, check to make sure you're getting more cheese than rind, since you're buying it by weight—you don't want half your cost to be in rind. That said, rinds are wonderful additions to soups (see pages 104–119) and risotti (see pages 90–103) during cooking, so hold on to them—Tuscans don't waste anything!

SALTED CAPERS AND ANCHOVIES: In the world of ways to salt dishes, these are two wonderfully flavorful alternatives. Especially when you want a seasoning kick that's a little more textural, capers and anchovies are great options.

OLIVES: We love the rich, large, pulpy fruit from southern Italy known as **Cerignola olives**, marinated very simply in olive oil, or sometimes in a more complex blending of orange, herbs, and spices. Our favorite olives to marinate are the small, black **Gaeta olives**, which make for great appetizers or a salty touch to a salad. The mild, green, Sicilian **Castelvetrano olive** is a wonderful snack with a glass of wine.

BEANS: Cannellini beans are an incredibly versatile Tuscan staple that have a butteriness and creaminess that complement many dishes.

Whether on bruschetta (page 39), in soup, or accompanying sausages (page 147), a can of these is a pantry item you'll be glad to have around. We are also fans of **borlotti beans**, which are large, red, and striped—we'll use them in tuna salads or soups, or slow-cook them in the fireplace as a side dish.

DRIED LENTILS: In Italy, lentils are a traditional holiday food, especially on New Year's Eve. We consider lentils as important as dried beans or split peas. We don't want to wait until year's end to enjoy them! They're great for soups, as a side dish, or in a salad.

POLENTA: Imported polenta from Italy is the way to go. As for whether to buy **regular polenta** or **instant polenta**, think about the level of commitment. The regular kind takes hours to prepare, with plenty of stirring involved, and occasional bubbles that thicken and pop. But if you're already working on a slow-cooked stew from scratch, it's a great textural accompaniment. We mostly use instant because of the time issues of feeding a family every day. It's quicker, thickens nicely, and we can mold and slice it or fry it as we see fit. And it's delicious!

PANCETTA AND GUANCIALE: These treasured cured-pig seasonings—pancetta from the pork belly and guanciale from the jowl—are our favorite way to imbue a dish with the essence of meat without actually bringing a hunk of pork to the table. Chopped into pieces no larger than a caper, and used as the basis for a sauce, their sudden appearance when you bite into a forkful of pasta is like a small gift of flavor that can elevate any eating experience. Plus, they freeze well.

WINE: We're not vino snobs. In most Tuscan restaurants, the *vino della casa*—or house wine—is what you drink throughout your meal, because it's from the local vineyard. It's invariably young and perfectly delicious. When it comes to cooking though, the general rule is to cook with **red wine** or **white wine** you would happily drink.

Of course, you won't be pouring a $40 Barolo into your stew dish. But in all instances, you'll be in good shape with a $15 to $20 bottle of imported Sangiovese or Chianti, ready to enhance your dish or to fill your glass while you cook.

Freezer items

The freezer can be your best friend, that special place that saves an exhausted home cook from having to come up with something new the next day. So not only do we keep quantities of essential items, we also have on hand frozen peas (for pastas), frozen spinach (for frittatas), frozen broccoli florets, Vegetable Stock (page 94) to thaw and use in soups and risottos, and an assortment of plastic containers filled with extra Sugo di Pomodoro (page 55), soups, and ragus.

Cooking Tools/Appliances/Vessels

We're big believers in spending money on great ingredients over expensive kitchen gadgets. If it feels good to you, use it, take care of it, and stick with it. It wouldn't surprise us if most big-time chefs, surrounded by the highest-end equipment at their jobs, still cooked at home with the pots, pans, utensils, and equipment they've been comfortable with for years. So this list is more of a guide than a directive. If we feel something is essential, it will be marked as such.

KNIVES: If you have a 9-inch and a 7-inch chef's knife, that's as good a start as any. Find one in that inch-range with a grip you like, and you'll be fine when it comes to most of your basic chopping, slicing, and carving. Other knives we've found useful for specific tasks in our kitchen are a 3-inch paring knife, a boning knife, a meat cleaver, and a serrated bread knife. For sharpening, we have a Wüsthof hand-held sharpener—the kind you run your knife through.

WOODEN UTENSILS: Wooden spoons—long and short—are often an extension of your hand: stirring, breaking up soft foods in a pan. Rolling pins come in large and small. We also like our wooden lemon juicer, the kind you hold in your hand as you ream the fruit. It cleans very easily. Our large, medium, and small rubber spatulas— good for baking, scooping out batters, and making cakes—have wooden handles.

METAL UTENSILS: We have long and short tongs, and metal spatulas that come in the angled, flat, and slotted variety. When it comes to whisks, it's good to have the standard kind and the balloon kind. The all-important ladle can be found in 8-ounce, 4-ounce, and 2-ounce versions, and you'll find plenty of large serving spoons in our kitchen. Potato mashers are useful, and we have vegetable peelers both traditional (swivel-bladed, stainless-steel) and Y-shaped (which slices thinly enough to double as a mandoline). For grating, we have a zester, a regular cheese grater, and a box grater we use on vegetables. Our kitchen shears come in handy for big cutting jobs.

STRAINERS/COLANDERS/FINE MESH SIEVE: When it comes to colanders, we prefer the kind with a pedestal base so the bottom of the straining bowl never has to touch the sink. If your sink is often full, or clogs easily, this kind is really helpful. For scooping food out of pots, we have a few spider strainers.

MEASURING TOOLS: We have one set of measuring spoons, and a set of plastic measuring cups for flour and sugar. Larger glass measuring cups are important, and we have them in 4-cup, 2-cup, and 1-cup sizes.

CUTTING BOARDS: You need good cutting boards. We have both plastic and wooden boards.

TIMER: A timer is essential, one that buzzes loud enough for you to hear even if you leave the kitchen.

BUTCHER'S TWINE: We have two rolls of butcher's twine for trussing meats.

INSTANT-READ THERMOMETER: This is a must, for either determining the doneness of meats, or checking the temperature of hot oil for frying.

IMMERSION BLENDER: Meet the appliance we use the most: the handheld Cuisinart immersion blender. We use it to emulsify sauces and dressings, and to blend peeled tomatoes for sauces and soups. We love it because we can detach the bottom part, rinse it, dry it, and stick it in a drawer. It saves us from transferring food in and out of a huge mixer or blender, which then becomes a pain to clean. Trust us on this one: This is *the* sound gadget investment!

STAND MIXER: We've just told you how much we hate cleaning these, yet here we are recommending it. But oh, the things you can do! The attachments are wonderful, a mini-lab at your disposal. We have one for grinding meat, making pasta, and have the dough hook and paddle attachments.

FOOD PROCESSOR: We wish we had the time to apply the ancient technique of grinding, crushing, and pulverizing with a mortar and pestle, but we have kids. We need to press a button and move on.

STOVETOP TOASTER: This flat tool for toasting bread is one way you can really show your friends how Italian you've become. When I gave one as a gift to our friend Margy, she said it looked like a space-age fan for a robot Geisha. It's a perforated grate with a handle that you place over high heat on your gas stove for grilling bread. It's commonplace in Italy (called **"La Gratella"**), and has started to make inroads in America, so be the first on your block to make bruschetta or even your morning toast this way!

PIZZA STONE: This is the flat stone (sometimes ceramic) that's used often in pizza-making and baking. Our pizza stone lives in our oven, no matter what we cook. It works well for everything, helping to diffuse heat properly and develop a core temperature. If we're baking a lasagne, we'll just put the pan on top of it.

PASTA MACHINE: If using a rolling pin feels too daunting, spend a little extra money on this product and get the solid steel, hand-cranked kind.

SAUCEPANS: We suggest 1.5-quart, 2-quart, and 2.5-quart saucepans, with lids.

SAUTÉ PANS/SKILLETS: An 8-inch, 10-inch, 12-inch, and 14-inch pan should do the trick.

STOCKPOTS: Either a 12-quart or 16-quart stockpot will get the job done for your stocks, while a pot in the 8- to 10-quart range should handle your pasta and soup needs.

ROASTING PANS/DUTCH OVENS: Le Creuset is king when it comes to these necessary items. Their 6- and 8-quart cast iron Dutch ovens are great, as are their roasting pans: We have a 14 × 10-inch and a 12 × 9-inch. Lodge makes wonderful cast iron pots, too.

BAKING DISHES/SHEETS: We recommend one 7 × 11-inch baking dish, as well as a 9 × 13-inch. For sheets, we have on hand a 13 × 18-inch and a 9 × 13-inch, both rimmed.

appetizers

ANTIPASTI

D: If we think of a table as something to be set before a meal, Italians think of their stomachs in the same way. The antipasto—literally "before the meal" in Italian—is that very course, the one that excites you and prepares you for the deliciousness that will follow. Although, as we like to joke, it's often an excuse to drink more wine.

Appetizers are almost celebratory. When we have guests, there's that initial thrill of seeing a table filled with cured meat, cheese, olives, bread, and good olive oil, and watching everybody dig in as the conversation revs up. It's the opener not just for your stomach, but the talking. The dishing before the main dish!

In Italy, appetizers are not about getting stuffed with food. If you're entertaining, it's about creating in your house that little corner where people keep going to meet each other. We love how a piece of cheese or a crostini with a smear of fresh ricotta can spark an exchange between two people.

G: I remember days in Italy, especially during Christmas, when relatives stayed at our house. The whole day—all the meals—were tied together by what was on the appetizer table. Let's say your parents are in town, or friends are visiting for the weekend: If after lunch the cheese and the cold cuts and the dried apricots stay on the table—and the wine stays open—it keeps the buzz of entertaining alive, and eventually culminates in a delicious dinner.

D: Of course, pacing can be an issue. If it's just a few people over for dinner, saving everyone's appetite for the main course—or courses—is important. What helps people stay honest at our house is that they're eating their salumi and cheese—or their bruschetta, or their crostini, or

whatever—while their noses are also detecting what's going on in the kitchen. Knowing that a roast is coming, or a fragrant pasta sauce is on the way, certainly helps keep their appetites in check. Or if they say hi in the kitchen, always a favorite spot to hang out before the formality of sitting down, they can actually see what's on the stove, and that usually puts an appropriate halt to the possible overconsumption of appetizers.

G: Appetizers can also act as a meal, which is why any of the antipasti recipes in this book just as easily work as an entree if you're thinking about a small lunch, or—if you had a big meal earlier in the day—whipping up a lighter dinner that won't fill you up all over again. What I love about our antipasti recipes is that while they're great for those times when you're entertaining and you want the many-course experience, they also double as healthy ways to placate hungry kids in the afternoon or as a simpler, less-complicated dinner.

Tuscans are famous for not liking to waste anything, so it's also important to remember that your leftovers can act as appetizers. The spinach from the night before becomes the spinach frittata that you eat for the next day's breakfast or snack. This kind of thinking allows you to be creative with bruschetta and crostini, too.

So consider these recipes as highly adaptable dishes, ready to delectably tease your guests with the leisurely, flavorful evening to follow, or to meet the snacking needs of a hungry family between meals.

HEIRLOOM TOMATO AND BURRATA CAPRESE

CAPRESE DI BURRATA E COSTOLUTO FIORENTINO

(pictured on page 18)

⸱ **SERVES 4** ⸱

G: *This staple of my childhood depends on the perkiness and freshness of the ingredients. Because it's so simple, its components need to be superb. The tomatoes have to be ripe, sliced thick but not too thick, and the cheese has to be soft and creamy. Burrata, which is cream and mozzarella enclosed in a sack made of mozzarella, is literally translated as "buttery." It's a classic for a reason, so don't settle for less. Use burrata made from mozzarella di bufala, which is by nature more supple, more yielding, and exquisitely delicious.*

2 heirloom tomatoes

1 pound burrata

Extra virgin olive oil, for serving

Kosher salt and freshly ground
　black pepper

8 fresh basil leaves, torn by hand

Cut the tomatoes into ¼-inch-thick slices, then dice 4 slices and set those aside for garnish. On a large plate, arrange the tomato slices, slightly overlapping, to cover the entire surface.

Place your thumbs on top of the burrata and open it gently. Place the burrata in the center of the plate, on top of the tomatoes.

Pour the diced tomato on top, and dress with extra virgin olive oil. Season with salt and pepper to taste, then sprinkle the basil leaves over the top.

IMPORTANTE! Serve with a slice of Tuscan bread and a glass of young wine, and you have a fresh, healthy lunch.

MOZZARELLA, TOMATO, AND FARRO SALAD

CAPRESE DI FARRO

D: *I love my farro. When I met my husband and I visited his mother for the first time, she made a farro salad, with tomatoes, fresh parsley, lemon, onion, and white beans, and it was so light, refreshing, and health-conscious I knew I'd met a kindred spirit. I learned that this ancient grain was eaten by Egyptians and Romans and is one of Italy's heritage foods, so its history as a sustaining source of nutrients runs deep. The northwest side of Tuscany—namely a town called Lucca—has the best farro we've tried, but you should be able to find farro easily at your local gourmet food store or online. This nutty salad is perfect for summertime and easy to prepare. Even if you overcook the farro, don't worry. Farro is forgiving and won't glue up or get sticky like rice.*

Kosher salt

1 pound farro

10 ounces cherry tomatoes, quartered

8 fresh basil leaves, torn by hand

1 (5-ounce) ball fresh mozzarella cheese, cut into ½-inch chunks

2 ounces pitted Kalamata olives

Extra virgin olive oil, for serving

Freshly ground black pepper

Bring a pot of salted water to a boil, toss in the farro, and cook for 20 minutes, until tender. Drain and rinse the farro with cold water.

Combine the farro, tomatoes, basil, mozzarella, and olives in a bowl. Drizzle with oil, then salt and pepper to taste.

Serve right away, or cover and refrigerate for the next day (this would be great for a picnic).

IMPORTANTE! Make sure you only use superior-grade mozzarella for this recipe. You are preparing a fresh salad, so stay away from the plastic-looking mozzarella blob sold at your regular grocery and find an establishment that carries the real deal.

OLIVE TAPENADE

TAPENADE DI OLIVE

G: *The Nostraline, or Tuscan olive, is revered in our culinary history, but it's really only good for oil because it's very small and the flavor is extremely pungent. They don't marinate as well as olives from the south of Italy, where there is more sun during the summer and the olives can get big, chunky, and rich with flavor. My mother's tapenade was made with store-bought olives marinated with orange zest, good olive oil, salt, and pepper. We'd then contrast the salty dominance of the olives with a wet, fresh taste, which is where the heirloom tomato comes in.*

D: *This makes for a beautiful look, too, when spread on a piece of bread. It's a form of bruschetta in a way. Making your own tapenade amounts to a lot of flavor.*

2 anchovy fillets

1 garlic clove, smashed

1 cup black Nostraline olives, pitted and roughly chopped

1 cup green Sicilian olives, pitted and roughly chopped

½ cup extra virgin olive oil, plus more for serving

1 tablespoon fresh lemon juice

2 tablespoons chopped fresh Italian parsley

½ tablespoon capers, rinsed and chopped

Toasted country bread slices, rubbed with raw garlic, for serving

1 heirloom tomato, sliced, for serving

Mash the anchovies with the garlic in a mortar and pestle, then mix well with the chopped olives. Combine with the ½ cup olive oil, the lemon juice, parsley, and capers.

Spread the tapenade on the garlic-rubbed toasts. Drizzle with olive oil and top with a slice of beautiful heirloom tomato.

PECORINO AND HONEY DIP

PECORINO E MIELE

─── • SERVES 6 • ───

D: *It doesn't get much easier to activate your guests' taste buds than this tried-and-true ménage à trois of salty, sweet, and hot. A good aged Pecorino will have the kind of granularity and tang that offsets the spiced-up honey. I have to confess that this was a pretty easy way for Gabriele to impress me when we first met, so maybe save this for your significant other, or that certain someone you've convinced should come over for a home-cooked meal. Add a glass of young Chianti and you're good to go. It's a suggestive starter in just the right way, especially with something as naturally drippy as honey! Just don't forget you might have a roast going in the kitchen. . . .*

¼ cup good-quality organic honey, for dipping

Pinch of hot red pepper flakes

½ pound aged Pecorino (such as Sardo or Pienza), cut into 2-inch-long, ½-inch-thick sticks

In a small bowl, stir together the honey and red pepper flakes. Serve with the Pecorino to dip into the honey.

PROSCIUTTO AND MELON

PROSCIUTTO E MELONE

· SERVES 4 ·

G: *My Jewish grandfather on my mother's side didn't care about keeping kosher. So when I was a young boy at the beach with my grandparents—and my observant doctor father was still working at the hospital—I got to enjoy this classic combo of porky salt-iness and fruity sweetness. Other times, when my dad was around, I'd look down the table and see Nonno Renato openly enjoying his forkful of prosciutto and cantaloupe. Then he'd just smile and wink at me. This can be an ideal kickoff to a barbecue, or—my favorite—a dish of Spaghetti alle Vongole (page 85).*

1 cantaloupe or Tuscan melon

½ pound prosciutto di Parma, thinly sliced

Halve the melon lengthwise. Using a spoon, scoop out the seeds. Then slice 6 wedges out of each half and remove the rinds.

Arrange the 12 wedges on a platter and drape 1½ slices of prosciutto on top of each cantaloupe slice. Serve.

IMPORTANTE! We find this to be especially delicious served with freshly brewed iced tea with a sprig of mint in it.

GUACAMOLE
with baked beet chips

BARBABIETOLE CROCCANTI E GUACAMOLE

———— • SERVES 8–12 • ————

D: *I'm the queen of guacamole, and my first house in Los Angeles featured an avocado tree with many loyal, delicious subjects. So when Gabriele moved in with me, he was introduced to my wonderfully chunky, addictive guacamole.*

G: *I had to Tuscanize it, of course, which is where the olive oil comes in. To me, olive oil always helps when making something soft and spreadable. I love avocados, but where I'm from, they're imported from Africa or Sicily, so they'd arrive at the store as hard as a rock, and you'd have to wait two weeks for them to ripen.*

D: *Gabriele's mother will actually buy them in advance for me when she knows we're coming to Italy, because I like to use them so much. That is so sweet. As for the beet chips, they're my version of a fun, nutritious way for kids to eat guacamole. Sliced thinly enough, they get a nice crunch, plus the pink color is always a hit.*

GUACAMOLE
SERVES 8

4 ripe medium Hass avocados, peeled and pitted

¼ red onion, diced (about ⅓ cup)

1 small tomato, diced

¼ cup fresh lime juice

2 tablespoons extra virgin olive oil

¼ cup coarsely chopped fresh cilantro

Sea salt and freshly ground black pepper

Baked Beet Chips (recipe follows) or store-bought fried beet or tortilla chips

In a large bowl, mash the avocados with a fork or potato masher to achieve a slightly chunky consistency. Add the onion, tomato, lime juice, olive oil, and cilantro, and stir to combine well. Season with salt and pepper to taste. Serve in a bowl with Baked Beet Chips.

IMPORTANTE! Cilantro can be a polarizing ingredient—either you love its aromatic qualities or you don't. For less cilantro punch, feel free to leave it out, or use some at the end as a garnish instead of mixing it in.

BAKED BEET CHIPS
SERVES 8–12

6 medium to large red beets

¼ cup extra virgin olive oil

Freshly ground black pepper and salt

Preheat the oven to 300°F.

Rinse and scrub the outside of the beets. Using a mandoline, carefully slice the beets into ¹⁄₁₆-inch-thick rounds and place in a large bowl. Drizzle with the olive oil, turning to coat the slices evenly. Place the beet slices in single layers on a baking sheet (or 2 if necessary) and season with pepper to taste (don't add the salt yet, as it will make the chips less crisp).

Bake for 30 to 45 minutes, rotating the baking sheet halfway through, until the slices are darkened around the edges and mostly crisp. Remove from the oven and let cool. The beets will firm up even more during cooling. They will also have shrunk by half. Once cooled, transfer the chips to a large bowl and toss with salt to taste. Serve with Guacamole (opposite).

IMPORTANTE! If using a convection oven, the chips will bake faster and get crispier. Preheat the oven to 400°F and bake for 12 to 15 minutes.

GRILLED APRICOTS
with goat cheese ricotta

ALBICOCCHE GRIGLIATE CON RICOTTA DI CAPRA

— SERVES 12 —

D: *Our property in Fiesole, Italy, is filled with wild apricot trees, but there are also trees Gabriele planted with his father when he was four or five years old. It's so rewarding to go there every summer and see the trees producing buckets and buckets of glorious fruit. We even love seeing the dazzling emerald green beetles that fly around when the apricots ripen. This hot-season antipasto isn't as dessert-y as you'd think though, especially if you have the kind of tart apricots we grow. After quickly searing the apricots on a grill and pairing them with goat cheese ricotta, you get a soft, beautiful meeting of tangy and luscious that excites the palate.*

12 apricots (firm-ripe), halved and pitted

4 ounces fresh goat cheese ricotta

Freshly ground black pepper

Sprigs of fresh rosemary or mint,
    for garnish (optional)

Extra virgin olive oil, for drizzling
    (optional)

Sea salt (optional)

Preheat a grill to high heat or prepare a charcoal grill until the coals are bright red.

Lay the apricot halves cut-side down on the grill. Grill for 3 to 4 minutes, until the halves have solid grill marks and can still be removed easily without sticking. (If you try to remove them and they stick, let them be—they will release in time.)

Transfer the apricot halves to a platter, cut-side up. Top with spoonfuls of the ricotta, season with pepper, and garnish with rosemary or mint sprigs, if desired. You can also drizzle with extra virgin olive oil and sprinkle with sea salt before serving.

IMPORTANTE! This dish is best made with less ripe apricots, because a too-ripe apricot will fall apart during grilling.

GRILLED ASPARAGUS
wrapped with lardo

INVOLTINI GRIGLIATI DI ASPARAGI E LARDO

• SERVES 6 •

G: *I love wrapping vegetables in cold cuts—*involtini *are roll-ups in Italian cuisine— but you can't grill items like prosciutto or speck, because it turns the meat into something that resembles a big salty cracker.* Lardo *is different, because lardo can melt. Now before you start thinking, "Lard? Isn't that fat?" Yes, but lard is liquid fat and lardo is cured fatback, infused with herbs like rosemary, so it has texture, taste, and silkiness. You should be able to find lardo at your higher end, more gourmet-inclined grocery stores. The reason I like it with asparagus on the grill is because the cold, thin-sliced lardo crisps in the same time as it takes to grill the vegetable. You're left with a nicely seasoned, thin, crisp, buttery creamy wrap around a crunchy salted spear.*

1 bunch medium asparagus (about 24 spears), woody bottom ends removed

24 thin slices lardo (get extras as they tear easily)

Extra virgin olive oil, for drizzling

Kosher salt and freshly ground black pepper

Preheat a grill to medium-high heat.

Carefully wrap 2 asparagus with 1 or 2 pieces of lardo, overlapping as you go. (If your lardo is cut paper-thin, then 2 will be easier to work with; if thick, 1 slice should be sufficient.)

Lay the asparagus diagonally across the grill to keep it from falling through the grates, or use a grill basket if you have one. Grill, turning occasionally, for 8 to 10 minutes, until the asparagus is just tender and charred and the lardo has rendered and started to become crispy. Remove from the grill and set aside. Drizzle with the olive oil before serving. Season with salt and pepper to taste.

IMPORTANTE! It may look like the lardo is melting off of the asparagus as you cook it . . . be patient! It will eventually crisp up and stay put. You may want to make extras because these will go fast!

FRITTATA
with zucchini

FRITTATA DI ZUCCHINI E FIORI DI ZUCCA

———————————— SERVES 6–8 ————————————

D: *As much as the fried version of zucchini blossoms meant to our courtship in Italy (see page 36), the use of these delicate, delicious flowers in a frittata binds us as a family when we're at the farm in Fiesole. In the United States, a spinach frittata might be our Sunday breakfast, but in Italy in summertime we make use of the zucchini petals. In the morning, the flower of the zucchini is open, which makes it easier to pop out the stamen—the part you don't eat—and helps preserve the natural beauty of the petals you'll be using. If there's one thing we love about this dish, it's the architectural splendor of it, the kind of elegant, ceremonious tidbit that livens up a brunch, especially with a glass of Prosecco.*

6 large eggs

2 tablespoons whole milk

¼ cup freshly grated Parmigiano-Reggiano cheese

Fine sea salt and freshly ground black pepper

2 tablespoons extra virgin olive oil

1 shallot, finely chopped

1 medium or 2 small zucchini, medium diced

1 tablespoon unsalted butter

2 or 3 zucchini flowers (optional), stamen removed, torn in half (see Fried Squash Blossoms, page 36, for stamen removal process)

In a large bowl, beat together the eggs and milk. Add the Parmesan and salt and pepper to taste. Stir until combined.

In an 8- to 10-inch skillet, heat the olive oil over medium heat. Add the shallot and zucchini and cook for 3 to 4 minutes, until just beginning to soften. When the zucchini has softened and achieved a golden color, remove from the heat and add to the eggs. Stir until combined.

Using the same pan, add the butter and swirl until melted. Add the egg and zucchini mixture and top with the torn zucchini flowers (if using). Cover and cook over medium-low heat for 8 minutes, or until the edges begin to brown and the center has set and is puffed slightly. Serve immediately.

SEARED SCALLOPS OVER ENGLISH PEA PURÉE

CAPESANTE SCOTTATE CON PUREE DI PISELLI

• SERVES 4 •

D: *We find sea scallops to be awfully rich as an entree, but they make a great starter, a crisp, buttery beginning to a light fish entree. The English pea purée provides a nice smooth contrast to the creamy, pulpy goodness of the scallop. You should be able to find English peas year-round, but if you want a seasonal touch, go for a fava bean purée if it's spring or summer.*

1 cup English peas (fresh or frozen)

1 carrot

1 celery stalk

1 medium Yukon Gold potato

½ yellow onion, roughly chopped

Kosher salt and freshly ground
   black pepper

Grated zest of 1 lemon

1 teaspoon finely sliced fresh mint

1 tablespoon extra virgin olive oil

1 tablespoon unsalted butter

12 sea scallops

1 handful fresh chives, for garnish

In a medium pot, bring 6 cups water to a boil. Add the peas and cook for 4 to 5 minutes until tender. Keeping the water at a boil, remove the peas, drain them, and rinse under running water. Set aside.

To the boiling water, add the carrot, celery, potato, and onion. Reduce to a low boil and cook for about 30 minutes to flavor the broth. Remove the potato, peel it under running water, and cut it into chunks. Discard the carrot, celery, and onion.

In a blender, combine the peas, potato, and a couple of ladles of the broth. Season with salt and pepper to taste. Blend to a purée.

In a small bowl, mix together the lemon zest and mint. Set aside.

In a large nonstick skillet, heat the olive oil and butter over medium-high heat. Add the scallops and cook for 3 minutes, without moving them around too much, then flip them and cook for another 3 minutes, or until caramelized on the edges.

Place about 2 tablespoons of pea purée in the center of each of 4 serving plates. Then gently place 3 scallops on top. Sprinkle with the lemon-mint mixture and garnish the plate with a few chives.

IMPORTANTE! Pea purée should be served warm or at room temperature, never cold.

FRIED SQUASH BLOSSOMS

FIORI DI ZUCCA FRITTI

D: *Gabriele made this for me on our first date. I'd always loved zucchini, but wasn't aware that they produced these wonderful flowers that were delicate and strange-looking, like a burst of fire on the end of a torch. I cherished the idea of him taking these beautiful blossoms—straight from his garden—stuffing them with cheese, lightly frying them, and feeding them to me as if I were a bee being nourished by this tuft of nature.*

G: *If you're looking to fall in love in summer, there are few things more poetic than this dish.*

D: *And nothing hotter than a man making them for you!*

16 zucchini flowers

1 cup ricotta cheese (fresh is best)

2 teaspoons finely grated lemon zest

1½ cups all-purpose flour

1 handful fresh Italian parsley, finely chopped

Kosher salt and freshly ground black pepper

1 (12-ounce) bottle lager beer

Vegetable oil, for frying

Use your fingers to carefully dig a hole on the side of each zucchini flower, opening it enough with your pointer finger to dig out the stamen that is inside. Gently rinse the flowers under a sprinkle of cold water, taking care to not damage the thin petals, then spread them out on a kitchen towel and gently pat dry.

In a medium bowl, mix together the ricotta and lemon zest. Fill a piping bag with the mixture. Carefully pipe 2 to 3 teaspoons of the ricotta mixture into each flower. Twist the petals to close tightly so the cheese won't escape during frying.

In a medium bowl, whisk together the flour, parsley, a couple of generous pinches of salt, and a few grinds of black pepper. Slowly start pouring the beer into the mixture, using a whisk or a fork to mix the batter, and work it enough to eliminate any lumps.

In a heavy skillet, pour in enough oil to come up a half inch, but no more than halfway up the sides. Heat the oil over high heat until a deep-fry thermometer reads 350°F.

Drag the flowers through the batter, making sure the batter does not get inside the flower, then slide into the hot oil. Fry for 2 minutes, flipping halfway through, until the blossom is golden and crisp. Then place them in a large dish on a couple of layers of paper towel to drain the excess oil. Salt to taste while the oil is still hot. Serve immediately.

BRUSCHETTA

We love the history that comes with this beloved antipasto. Born in the Middle Ages, it grew out of a peasant's need, rather than a cook's creativity. When the master of the house was finished eating—and that meant feeding his dog, too—then the servants would get to eat. They'd scrape the pans to collect the meal scraps, but they didn't have dishware or flatware. They would have to use stale bread, which was their plate and their utensil all in one. There's wonderful irony in what is now so versatile and civilized an appetizer having such poor, born-of-need origins. Leftovers on old bread may not sound like much, but it's lasted centuries for a reason. Nowadays you'll see restaurant bruschetta so unwieldy you need a fork to eat it, otherwise it'll fall apart. But ideally you should be able to pick it up and eat it.

Crostini are a form of bruschetta, a "little toast" designed to be held between two fingers and consumed in only one or two bites. It's that perfect party tray appetizer. You can also think of the difference between bruschetta and crostini this way: with the former, you spoon on the topping since your bread base is larger and possibly thicker, and with the latter's tinier real estate, you spread. With that in mind, we've chosen bruschetta and crostini recipes that highlight that difference in what can go on top.

WHITE BEAN AND PANCETTA BRUSCHETTA

BRUSCHETTA DI FAGIOLI E PANCETTA

· SERVES 8–10 ·

D: *Tuscans have historically been called Bean Eaters, because they have often clung to staples that last longer, like dried beans. In Tuscan culture, nothing gets tossed out. Tuscans have been known to eat beans every day of the week if they need to. And if it means more indulging in the round, buttery feel of cannellini beans when they're soft and lightly mashed, count us as Bean Eaters, too. We love these beans, especially with rosemary and olive oil.*

2 tablespoons extra virgin olive oil, plus more for serving

¼ pound pancetta, diced

3 sprigs fresh rosemary, leaves removed

2 garlic cloves, thickly sliced

2 (15-ounce) cans cannellini beans, drained and rinsed

Squeeze of lemon juice

Kosher salt and freshly ground black pepper

1 day-old baguette, cut into ¾-inch-thick slices

Heat a fireplace grill to a medium heat. Adjust grill racks over the flame and place a heavy Dutch oven or medium saucepan on the rack. Once hot, add the 2 tablespoons olive oil to the pan. Then add the pancetta and render some of its fat. Add the rosemary and garlic and sauté until fragrant. Stir in the beans, lemon juice, and salt and pepper to taste. Mash the beans with the back of the wooden spoon, but don't mash until smooth—you want some texture.

Toast the sliced baguette. Serve the beans on top of the toasted bread. Drizzle with olive oil, if desired.

LARDO CROSTINI

CROSTINI DI LARDO

G: *I love getting my hands into this appetizer, mashing the chunks of lardo with the herbs, until it's this perfectly spreadable paste.*

D: *This is what happens at our house when people pop these crostini into their mouths: Eyes roll back, lips part slightly, and you hear moaning. "Hmmmm . . ." "Ohhhh . . ." It's like we're hosting a swinging singles party. Suddenly there's a very orgasmic vibe wafting through our home.*

G: *Sex noises are good, no?*

D: *Well, as long as there are multiple climaxes, meaning you've got room for a pasta or an entree that's just as delicious! Nobody wants premature . . . um . . . meal satisfaction, let's say.*

G: *In all seriousness, lardo is naturally heavy, so it's very important that you have a later course that balances the richness of cured pork fat with something lighter, like Pici all'Aglione (page 56).*

½ pound lardo, at room temperature

1 tablespoon fresh rosemary leaves, finely chopped

4 or 5 fresh sage leaves, finely chopped

Grated zest of 1 small lemon

Kosher salt and freshly ground black pepper

1 baguette, thinly sliced

Using a sharp knife, very finely chop the lardo. Add the rosemary, sage, and lemon zest. Season with salt and pepper to taste and mix well with the back of your knife or your hands.

Spread on the baguette slices.

FRESH CHEESE CURD CROSTINI

CROSTINI DI CAGLIATA FRESCA

In making the soft, pillowy cheese known as ricotta, *there are two steps. (That's why* ricotta *means "recooked" in Italian.) The first step, when you add citric acid or rennet to whole milk, yields* cagliata, *which is the first separation of curds from whey, and it makes for a delicious crostini spread all on its own. It's creamier and richer than ricotta, since the second step is a further cooking of the whey that gets you the lighter, airier taste associated with ricotta. We're putting on the brakes at the cagliata stage, however, because we think it deserves a spotlight of its own!*

4 cups whole milk

3 tablespoons fresh lemon juice

½ teaspoon kosher salt

1 baguette, thinly sliced and toasted

1 teaspoon grated lemon zest

Extra virgin olive oil, for serving

Line a colander with 3 layers of cheesecloth.

In a large, heavy pot, bring the milk to a simmer over medium-high heat. Stir in the lemon juice and salt and heat until an instant-read thermometer reaches 175°F. The milk will begin to just bubble and start to steam. At this temperature you'll begin to see the curds separate from the whey.

Remove from the heat and stir for up to 5 minutes. Be mindful of overstirring while the curds are forming—you don't want to make your cheese tough. Let sit for 5 minutes undisturbed and you will be left with a pleasantly creamy result.

Gently pour the curds into the colander, and very gently release some of the liquid. Tie the cheesecloth in a sack using butcher's twine, lift the sack from the colander, and let drain without squeezing for 5 to 10 minutes, or until liquid stops seeping out. Remove the curds from the cheesecloth and place in a bowl.

Spread warm on toasted bread with a sprinkling of lemon zest and a drizzle of extra virgin olive oil.

IMPORTANTE! You can refrigerate leftover cagliata in a covered container for up to 5 days.

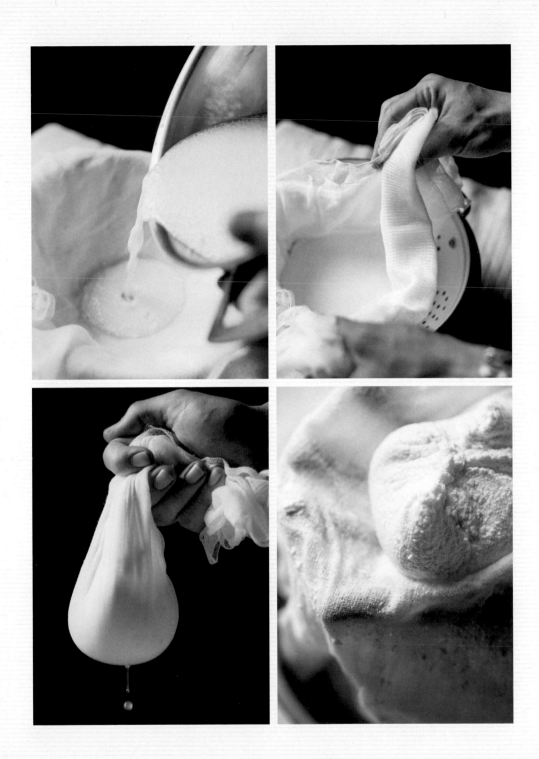

STRIPED BASS CRUDO TRIO

TRIO DI BRANZINO CRUDO

— SERVES 4 —

G: *For me, summer with my parents on the coast of Tuscany in Castiglioncello was about the fishing I got to do, three to six hours every day in the water with spears and a snorkel. I typically caught our dinner: sole, cuttlefish, sea bass, whatever was in my line of sight. I'd gut the fish, scale it, then cook it. But I would often try it raw, too, and I have to say, there's a primal enjoyment to eating something from the sea that was only alive mere moments before. This recipe comes from my time designing a menu for the Montauk Yacht Club, when I did my first deep-sea fishing in the Atlantic and caught a 38-pound striped bass. It was big enough to slice very thin and I turned it into a trio of raw, ocean goodness, complemented by flavors like lemon, orange, red pepper flakes, and shallots. It was an immediate hit, and goes very nicely before a pasta like l'Aragosta Arrabbiata (page 82). Remember that the slicing can be done well in advance, up to 4 hours, as long as it's refrigerated.*

½ pound striped bass (or other sushi-grade fish), skin removed

3 ounces cold-smoked fish, preferably striped bass

4 teaspoons fresh lemon juice

1 teaspoon grated lemon zest

12 leaves fresh flat-leaf Italian parsley, coarsely chopped

1 orange, supremed, juices reserved (see note)

1 teaspoon hot red pepper flakes

1 teaspoon lightly chopped fennel fronds

½ cup halved heirloom cherry tomatoes (mixed colors)

½ shallot, minced

2 tablespoons Vin Santo

Sea salt and freshly ground black pepper

Extra virgin olive oil, for drizzling

Chill 4 plates.

Slice the raw bass paper-thin, on a slight bias and against the grain of the fish. Depending on how thinly you slice, you should have between 16 and 24 slices. Arrange the slices in two separate groupings of 2 to 3 slices on each of the chilled plates. This is two parts of the crudo trio.

For the third part of the trio, thinly slice (or, if easier, flake) the smoked fish into 12 to 20 pieces and divide into 4 portions. Add to the chilled plates.

On each plate, sprinkle 1 teaspoon lemon juice, ¼ teaspoon lemon zest, one-quarter of the coarsely chopped parsley, and one quarter of the reserved juices over one of the groupings of sliced bass.

In a small bowl, combine the orange segments, red pepper flakes, and fennel fronds. Stir to combine. Spoon 3 orange segments over each second grouping of sliced bass.

In another small bowl, combine the tomatoes, shallot, and Vin Santo. Stir to combine and spoon over each grouping of the smoked fish.

Lightly season each fish grouping with salt and pepper to taste. Top with a drizzle of finishing extra virgin olive oil. Serve immediately.

IMPORTANTE! Supreming is a way of extracting the juiciest, purest segments from a fruit, and an easy technique to master. Using a sharp knife, trim the top and bottom of the orange (by either a ¼-inch or ½-inch). Do this over a bowl to capture the juices. Then, carefully cut away the peel, making sure to remove the pith just under the peel as well. (Do this by cutting from the top down.) Then, remove the wedges by cutting as close to the white membrane as possible, through the fruit to the center, then following through along the very next membrane. This should result in nice, juicy-looking segments.

pasta and sauces
PASTA E SUGHI

D: Gabriele and I believe that pasta brings a family together at mealtime like no other food. We get so much enjoyment out of the looks on our daughters' faces when they dig into their favorite pastas that sometimes it feels like that bowl of shells and pesto, or penne and red sauce, is as Italian a way of saying "I love you" as blurting out "Ti amo!"

G: Pasta is at the heart of so many of our fondest memories. For me it's being twelve years old and making spaghetti and meat sauce on Saturday nights for me and my brother when our parents would go out with friends.

D: For me it's having a connection with my mother and grandmother by way of a big bowl of well-sauced rigatoni. Pasta is the best comfort food, and when I met my husband, it quickly dawned on me how much the Tuscans think of that comfort food in terms of simplicity, freshness, and the balance of ingredients. You won't find vodka and cream sauces or overcheesed, overloaded pastas in Tuscany. Where Gabriele grew up it was about that melding of herbs, or the drizzle of olive oil, or the spark of flavor that garlic and pancetta bring.

G: And yes, pasta has carbs, which have had a rough go of late in the often diet-obsessed American culture. But pasta can also bring healthy vegetables to your kids' mouths, or protein-rich meats—and since we all need carbs at some point anyway, wouldn't you rather carbs be delivered to your children by way of delicious, life-affirming pasta?

DRIED VERSUS FRESH

In Italy, the conversation is never about whether to make tricolore (tri-colored) pasta, or whole wheat pasta, or gluten-free pasta. To Italians, that isn't pasta. It's a question of dried versus fresh, and even then the answer can only come when you know what sauce you're making. Something as simple as a Red Sauce (page 55) or a Carbonara (page 74) goes well with perfectly cooked dried pasta, and if you stick to sturdy, reliable imported Italian brands like De Cecco and Barilla, you'll be in good shape. Whereas if you're spending hours on a succulent Duck Ragu (page 72) or highlighting an in-season

vegetable like porcini mushrooms, you might want the more complementary taste of a softer, silkier handmade noodle. Plus, taking that extra time to make with your own hands something that brings such enjoyment to people is often worth the effort.

SHAPES

Since pasta is a vehicle, the construction and shape of your pasta has the power to literally and figuratively "transport" your sauce. If your sauce is chunky and meaty, a pasta with the ability to capture it, like shells (conchiglie, lumaconi, orecchiette), spirals (fusilli), or ridged tubes

(rigatoni, penne rigate), works best. With the classic strand pastas like spaghettis, we love their ability to hold oil-based sauces like Aglio e Olio (page 57), a wine-infused seafood sauce such as Vongole (page 85), or tomato sauces if using a thicker variety of strand pasta like bucatini.

COOKING PASTA

How much water you want to use when boiling it for pasta is up to you, but a good rule is 6 quarts per pound of pasta, although you can cook up to 2 pounds in that amount of water, too. (For every 1 pound after that, increase the water amount by 2 quarts.) The less water you use though, the more you need to pay attention to it to ensure the pieces don't stick together. Don't fall for the pervasive myth that adding olive oil or butter to a pot of water prevents pasta from sticking together. All the oil will do is sit on the surface of the water, go straight down the drain when you pour the water out, and if anything, work against your pasta adhering to the sauce you've made, which is the "sticking" you want! The only tried-and-true technique is stirring your pasta a few times as it cooks, and most important, right after the pasta goes into the boiling water.

As for salting, remember that pasta by itself is fairly flavorless, which is why you salt the water *before* adding the pasta. Think of it as getting ready for a hot date: a pasta giving off its own unique flavor thanks to the salt can only help attract the savoriness of a sauce waiting to be approached. Two good pinches of salt (or about 1 tablespoon) is all it takes. We prefer salting the water even before turning on the flame underneath the pot. If you've oversalted your pasta, it's not the end of the world. You can quickly rinse it in warm water in a strainer after you've drained it.

What you're looking for from your dried pasta in terms of doneness is what's called *al dente*, meaning "to the tooth," which lets you know that it's firm and slightly chewy, but thoroughly cooked. This requires setting the timer to go off a couple of minutes before the box recommends, then start tasting it early. The moment it's al dente—boom—rescue your pasta from the water. Remember that in many instances you'll be cooking it a tad further when it gets added to your sauce, so even pasta the tiniest bit underdone will get a chance to reach its ideal texture once wedded to the sauce. We're all our best selves, after all, once we meet that special partner, no?

Lastly, with most of the following dishes, we implore you not to let your cooked, naked pasta sit in bowls, waiting for sauce to be plopped on top. You see that so often in commercials, or on packaging: the white pasta with what looks like ladled soup on it. It's not appetizing. Toss your just-cooked, quickly drained pasta in your sauce and let the two enjoy their first bonding, if only for 30 seconds or a minute. (One exception is ragus, which tend to get placed atop pasta in the bowl because of their natural thickness.) Save some of the pasta water, too, for those moments when a splash of the starchy liquid might help "loosen" the grip your sauce has on the pasta. Your marriage of pasta and sauce—much like the human kind of matrimony—should be close and comforting, but not suffocating!

THE SOFFRITTO

G: Throughout the pasta recipes, and in many of the sauce-heavy or stewlike dishes in this book, you'll see that the steps often start with extra virgin olive oil heated up, followed by the sautéing of herbs and/or vegetables. This first burst of aromatic flavor is what we call the *soffritto*. It comes from the Italian herb *soffriggere*, which means "to fry lightly." Think of it as the prologue to your dish, the way you set the tone. (Or, if we're thinking passionately, the back rub before things move from the couch to the bedroom!) It might be garlic and olive oil for a red sauce, or a mixture of onions, carrots, and celery for something more complicated.

I remember these books from when I was growing up that allowed the reader to make decisions in the middle of the story that could take you in different directions. If you opted to open one door as opposed to another, you turned to a specific page to see what happened. Soffrittos are similar, in that when you start with, say, olive oil and garlic, you have a wide range of possibilities for your dish. But as soon as you add hot red pepper flakes, you've narrowed it down to pastas, not stews. If you

added anchovies though, you might be headed in the direction of a chicken cacciatore. With each ingredient, the adventure gets more specific, and your recipe starts to come together to form that unique, one-of-a-kind dish.

The soffritto is the base, in other words, and it's important enough of a concept that if you realize you've burned the garlic, or let the onions discolor, don't get upset. Just start again, and give it the attention it deserves. Better to restart a soffritto than let compromised flavors affect the dish later. You'll become a more confident kitchen maestro, your home will come alive with fantastic aromas, and the ending to your multiple-ingredient story will be apparent in the happy faces of the people you're cooking for.

Soffritto mainstays (keep these ingredients well-stocked!): extra virgin olive oil, garlic, carrots, celery, onion, shallots, hot red pepper flakes, pancetta, and guanciale.

HANDMADE PAPPARDELLE

PAPPARDELLE FATTE IN CASA

MAKES 1 POUND

One of the big draws of making your own pasta is the feeling you get working with your hands, which is why Gabriele's grandmother didn't like to use a pasta machine. She liked how that marble pin felt as she crafted her exquisite batches of pasta. So we suggest you skip the pasta machine part and roll the dough on a big surface until you achieve the thickness you want. You might surprise yourself with how much you enjoy making your own fresh pasta! Serve the pappardelle with either a delicious Duck Ragu (page 72) or hearty "Fake" Sauce (page 59).

3½ cups all-purpose flour, plus more for rolling

¾ teaspoon salt, plus more for the pasta pot

4 large eggs, preferably farm fresh, lightly beaten

1 teaspoon extra virgin olive oil

Semolina flour, for dusting

Add the flour and salt to the center of a large wooden board. Use your hands and make a well in the center of the mound. In a bowl, whisk together the eggs and olive oil and pour into the well. Use a fork to slowly mix the eggs into the flour until they are completely incorporated.

(continued)

Knead the pasta dough for about 8 minutes, adding flour in small increments if the board gets sticky. If the dough feels too dry, add 1 teaspoon of water occasionally as you go. The dough should feel elastic and smooth. Shape the pasta dough into a ball and cover it in plastic wrap. Let rest for at least 30 minutes at room temperature to let the gluten relax. This will make the rolling easier.

Set your pasta machine to the widest setting. Divide the dough into 4 pieces. Roll each piece through the machine, from the widest setting to the thinnest. Hand-cut the pasta into pappardelle—strips about 3/4 inch wide and 10 inches long.

Gather the pappardelle in your hands and shake them loose so the strands don't stick together. Toss with some semolina flour. Divide into separate serving portions on a baking sheet. (This also helps to prevent the pasta from sticking together.)

Bring a large pot of salted water to a boil. Add the pasta and cook for 3 minutes, or until al dente. Drain.

IMPORTANTE! Fresh pasta is best enjoyed the same day you make it. If you've made the pappardelle in the morning, you can keep it divided into serving portions on a baking sheet covered with a kitchen towel, preferably in a cool area, before cooking it for lunch or dinner. Although not ideal, if you intend to eat it the next day, keep it in the refrigerator overnight on a baking sheet dusted with semolina flour.

RED SAUCE

SUGO DI POMODORO

MAKES 2 CUPS
(ENOUGH FOR 1 POUND OF PASTA)

D: *When I was a child, my grandmother became a great Italian cook partly because she had a Sicilian boyfriend. Naturally, she had a killer red sauce, but when I first made it for my new Tuscan beau, Gabriele, it was obviously the kind he didn't grow up with: heavy on garlic, and loaded with everything from carrots to beef to pork sausage, plus tomato paste to thicken it. It even had sugar, and if we felt like making it creamy, we'd add ricotta cheese on top. I quickly learned from the horrified expression on Gabriele's face that this more Southern-Italian version wasn't what he considered a sauce.*

Gabriele's grandmother, meanwhile, was making something much simpler and fresher, the result of tomatoes picked from the garden, run through the mill, cooked for hours, and then jarred for use over months and months. When Gabriele introduced me to his family red sauce recipe, it was like heaven had arrived. When done right, a red sauce like this can make you feel alive.

1 (28-ounce) can whole peeled tomatoes (pelati)

2 tablespoons extra virgin olive oil

⅓ red onion, medium diced

3 garlic cloves, cut into chunks

Pinch of hot red pepper flakes (optional)

Salt and freshly ground black pepper

2 tablespoons torn fresh basil

In a food processor, or using an immersion blender, purée the tomatoes to a smooth creamy consistency. (If you like a more country feel, you can wait and break them up in the pan later with a wooden spoon.)

In a large saucepan, heat the olive oil over medium-high heat until hot. Add the onion and sauté 5 to 6 minutes, or until soft. Add the garlic and cook for 2 to 3 minutes, until you see the color start changing. If you'd like to make the sauce spicy, add the red pepper flakes.

Add the tomatoes and season with salt and black pepper to taste. Reduce the heat to medium-low and simmer for about 30 minutes. (If you did not purée the tomatoes, use a wooden spoon to break them into pieces while they cook.) Strive for balance in the consistency of the sauce. It has to be fluid, but it should not look overly wet. Add the basil and remove from the heat.

PICI ALL'AGLIONE

D: *Aglione is a garlic-loaded red sauce—ideally your garlic count is one clove per person. It's wonderful with pici, a traditional hand-rolled spaghetti from Siena, and if you look online you should be able to buy it. But thick spaghetti works just as well.*

Kosher salt

2 tablespoons extra virgin olive oil

4 to 6 garlic cloves (1 per person!)

1 fresh chile, such as red serrano, sliced, or more to taste

1 (28-ounce) can whole peeled tomatoes (pelati), crushed by hand

Freshly ground black pepper

1 pound pici or thick spaghetti

Fresh basil leaves, for garnish

In an 8- to 12-quart pot, bring 6 quarts of salted water to a rolling boil.

In a large skillet, heat the olive oil over medium-high heat until hot. Add the garlic and chile(s). When the garlic becomes fragrant, after 3 to 5 minutes, add the crushed tomatoes and cook for 20 minutes until reduced to a sauce. Season with salt and black pepper to taste and remove from the heat.

Add the pici to the boiling water and use a wooden fork to stir the pasta so it won't stick together. Cook until al dente. Ladle out ½ cup of the pasta water, then drain the pasta.

Add the pasta to the sauce, toss together, and cook over medium heat for 1 minute. Add pasta water as needed to make the sauce slightly loose and glossy.

Serve immediately with the basil, and make sure each bowl gets its own garlic clove.

SPAGHETTI AGLIO E OLIO

D: *Light, spicy, quick, and sexy, this is something to make late at night with your loved one. Sometimes we'll come back from a night out, with the kids already in bed, and Gabriele will whip this up just for us. It's the food equivalent of an all-black-with-heels look in fashion: simple, but with a bold kick.*

Kosher salt

1 pound thick spaghetti

¼ cup extra virgin olive oil

3 garlic cloves, minced

2 teaspoons hot red pepper flakes, plus more to taste

Freshly ground black pepper

Bring a pot of salted water to a rolling boil and add the spaghetti. Use a wooden fork to stir the pasta so it won't stick together. Cook the pasta until al dente and drain.

Meanwhile, in a large serving bowl, mix together the olive oil, garlic, and red pepper flakes.

Add the drained pasta to the bowl and toss evenly to coat with the oil. Season with salt and black pepper to taste. Add more red pepper flakes if your palate calls for it.

IMPORTANTE! If raw garlic isn't to your liking, sauté it and the red pepper flakes in the olive oil in a large pan over high heat for 2 to 3 minutes. Add the cooked, drained pasta and continue cooking for a few minutes more over a high flame. Also, as much as you may want to, don't add Parmigiano-Reggiano. This pasta is about oil and heat, not cheese!

"FAKE" SAUCE

SUGO FINTO

Finto means fake, so this is a "fake" sauce: It originated with farmers who wanted the body and heartiness of a regular red sauce but couldn't afford the meat. The chunks of onion, carrot, and celery provide the meatlike texture, while the use of red wine gives it added color and depth. Of course, for all you vegetarians, lack of meat may make this more "real" for you than "fake"!

¼ cup extra virgin olive oil

½ red onion, roughly chopped

1 carrot, roughly chopped

2 celery stalks, roughly chopped

⅓ cup red wine

1 (28-ounce) can whole peeled tomatoes (pelati)

1 tablespoon finely chopped fresh Italian parsley, plus more for garnish

Kosher salt and freshly ground black pepper

Freshly grated Parmigiano-Reggiano cheese, for serving

In a large skillet, heat the olive oil over medium-high heat. Add the onion, carrot, and celery and cook for 5 to 7 minutes, until the onions are soft and golden, just before caramelization.

Add the red wine and stir well. Reduce the heat slightly and simmer for 5 minutes, or until the pungent smell of alcohol is gone.

Add the tomatoes and break them down roughly with a wooden spoon. Add the 1 tablespoon parsley and season with salt and pepper to taste. Stir well and cook over low heat for 30 to 40 minutes until the sauce thickens and the flavors blend.

Toss with 1 pound of just-cooked pasta and serve garnished with more parsley and grated Parmesan.

PASTA ALLA NORMA "NUDA"

· SERVES 4–6 ·

D: *The Norma is a traditional Sicilian pasta dish—named for the Bellini opera—that typically combines fried eggplant and ricotta. We removed the frying oil and cheese to make it a healthier, lighter-tasting, and "nuda" (naked) alternative that we think you'll love. Grilling the eggplant helps retain its density of character, too, and in summer Gabriele might go so far as to make the soffritto on the grill, using a heavy-bottomed pan.*

Kosher salt

2 tablespoons extra virgin olive oil, plus more for serving

½ small red onion, diced

Pinch of hot red pepper flakes

1 (15-ounce) can whole peeled tomatoes (pelati), crushed by hand

Freshly ground black pepper

1 medium eggplant, sliced into thin rounds

1 fresh bay leaf

1 pound rigatoni or fusilli

Fresh basil leaves, for garnish (optional)

Freshly grated Parmigiano-Reggiano cheese, for serving (optional)

Preheat the grill. In an 8- to 12-quart pot, bring 6 quarts of salted water to a boil.

In a large skillet, heat the olive oil over medium-high heat until hot. Add the onion and sauté for 4 to 5 minutes, until soft but before it starts to brown. Add the red pepper flakes and cook less than a minute, until they are fragrant but not burnt.

Add the tomatoes, season with salt and black pepper to taste, reduce the heat to medium-low, and simmer for 20 minutes. The sauce should be fluid but not wet and liquidy.

Meanwhile, season the eggplant with salt and pepper. Place on the grill, drizzle with olive oil, and cook 2 to 3 minutes per side, until cooked through. Remove from the heat to a large plate or baking sheet and allow to cool slightly.

Slice the eggplant into ½-inch-wide strips. Add the eggplant and bay leaf to the sauce and continue simmering for 5 minutes. Remove from the heat.

Add the pasta to the boiling water and use a wooden fork to stir the pasta so it won't stick together. Cook until al dente. Drain, add the pasta to the sauce, and toss well. Remove the bay leaf before serving. If desired, garnish with basil and top with Parmesan to taste.

SPAGHETTI PUTTANESCA

G: *The history of this salty, flavor-packed pasta often refers to its ladies-of-the-night origins, whereby crafty brothels would make this fragrant concoction to lure in customers. I prefer to think of it as the carbo-loading pick-me-up the women might have needed. One of the early energy foods, perhaps?*

1 pound tomatoes

Kosher salt and freshly ground
    black pepper

3 tablespoons extra virgin olive oil,
    plus more for serving

2 garlic cloves, sliced

4 anchovy fillets

Pinch of hot red pepper flakes

2 ounces Gaeta or Ponentine black olives,
    pitted and sliced

1 tablespoon capers, rinsed and chopped

1 pound spaghetti

Finely chopped fresh Italian parsley,
    for garnish

Bring a large pot of water to a boil. Submerge the tomatoes in the boiling water for 1 minute, then remove and peel them. Slice the tomatoes in half, remove the seeds, and cut into small cubes.

In an 8- to 12-quart pot, bring 6 quarts of salted water to a rolling boil for the pasta.

In a large skillet, heat the olive oil over medium-high heat until hot. Add the garlic, anchovies, red pepper flakes, olives, and capers and sauté for 3 to 4 minutes, so the flavors can meld. Use a wooden spoon to break up the anchovies. Add the tomatoes and cook over medium-low heat for 10 to 15 minutes. Season with salt and pepper to taste, being mindful that anchovies and capers play a big role in flavoring your puttanesca.

Add the spaghetti to the boiling water and use a wooden fork to stir the pasta so it won't stick together. Cook until al dente. Drain and add to the skillet. Toss well over medium-high heat for up to 2 minutes.

Serve with a sprinkle of parsley and a drizzle of olive oil.

PESTO

There are few culinary pleasures in life as fragrantly intoxicating as freshly made pesto, the Genovese-originated mixture of basil, pine nuts, olive oil, garlic, and cheese that—when made well—tastes even better than the promise of its sweet, nutty aroma. Though we're like any busy, money-minded family and make ours in a food processor, we suggest trying it at least once by combining the ingredients in a mortar and pestle. Pesto comes from the Italian word pestare—*to stomp—and when you grind everything by hand, you're squeezing out and blending oils and flavors in a way that produces something even more wonderfully rustic, aromatic, and possibly more delicious. As for pasta pairings, we suggest something with grooves that can trap the pesto, like fusilli or penne rigate. Also try it in Pesto Lasagne (page 68) for a lighter version of the classic.*

½ cup extra virgin olive oil

4 cups fresh basil leaves (about 4 ounces)

⅓ cup pine nuts, toasted

3 garlic cloves

½ cup freshly grated Parmigiano-Reggiano cheese

¼ cup freshly grated Pecorino Sardo or Romano cheese

Kosher salt and freshly ground black pepper

Using a mortar and pestle or in a food processor, combine the olive oil, basil, pine nuts, and garlic and blend until a paste forms. Add the Parmesan and Pecorino cheeses, and pulse until smooth.

Season with salt and pepper to taste. Be mindful that Pecorino and Parmesan are salty cheeses.

IMPORTANTE! When storing pesto in the refrigerator, add an extra layer of olive oil—that will help preserve its freshness and keep the color from turning to dark green too quickly. You can also freeze it.

LASAGNE ALLA BOLOGNESE

D: *In the Italian-American New York of my youth, lasagne was layer after heavy layer of sauce, meat, pasta, and cheeses, and treasured all the more because of that. The Bolognese version Gabriele and I love has plenty of meat, but calls for less cheese, and makes use of the creamy white sauce known as* besciamella. *This lasagne is so flavorful, light, and balanced that it can be its own entree, yet it won't cast a shadow over anything else in a multi-course menu, either. Seconds are a given!*

Butter, for greasing the baking dish

3 cups Bolognese (page 66)

1½ (9-ounce) boxes no-boil lasagna noodles

3 cups Besciamella (page 67)

¾ cup freshly grated Parmigiano-Reggiano cheese, plus more for serving

Extra virgin olive oil, for serving (optional)

Preheat the oven to 375°F.

Grease a 9 × 13-inch baking dish with butter. Spread a thin layer of the Bolognese (about ½ cup) over the bottom of the dish. Add the first layer of lasagne noodles to cover the meat sauce, being sure not to overlap the noodles. (Because you're working with no-boil noodles, each noodle piece should be covered with sauce, or else it won't cook!)

Add a layer of besciamella (a scant ¾ cup), then a generous sprinkle of Parmesan. Repeat the layering—Bolognese (about ¾ cup), noodles, besciamella, Parmesan—until you reach the top of the dish. The top layer should be a final thin spread of Bolognese and besciamella together. Finish with Parmesan.

Bake for about 30 minutes until bubbly and golden brown on top. For a nice crisp top, turn on the broiler and bake for another 5 minutes. Let rest for 5 minutes before serving. Keep extra virgin olive oil and Parmesan handy for a final garnish before serving.

(continued)

BOLOGNESE

MAKES 6 CUPS
(ENOUGH FOR TWO 9 × 13-INCH PANS OF LASAGNE)

5 tablespoons extra virgin olive oil

1 red onion, roughly chopped

3 carrots, roughly chopped

3 celery stalks, roughly chopped

5 ounces pancetta, cut into small cubes

1 pound ground beef

1 pound ground pork

1 pound ground veal

½ teaspoon hot red pepper flakes

2 tablespoons finely chopped fresh Italian parsley

1 cup red wine

3 (28-ounce) cans whole peeled tomatoes (pelati), puréed in a blender

Kosher salt and freshly ground black pepper

1 cup whole milk

In a 6- to 8-quart pot, heat the olive oil over medium-high heat until hot. Add the onion, carrots, celery, and pancetta and sauté for 10 to 12 minutes, or until the pancetta looks crisp and the vegetables have softened.

Add the beef, pork, and veal, increase the heat to high, and stir frequently, breaking up the meat until it is browned. Add the red pepper flakes and parsley and cook for 1 minute. Add the wine and cook for 4 to 5 minutes, until the alcohol is completely evaporated.

Add the puréed tomatoes, season generously with salt and pepper, then reduce the heat to medium and cook for 2 hours 30 minutes, stirring occasionally.

Add the milk, stir well, remove from the heat, and set aside to cool before using in the lasagne.

IMPORTANTE! Keep in mind that the Bolognese recipe on its own makes for a fantastic meat sauce to accompany any dried pasta—just leave out the whole milk!

BESCIAMELLA

MAKES 3 CUPS

2¼ cups whole milk

4 tablespoons (¼ stick) unsalted butter

¼ cup all-purpose flour

Pinch of freshly grated nutmeg

Kosher salt and freshly ground
   black pepper

In a small saucepan, warm the milk over medium heat.

In a medium skillet, melt the butter over medium heat. Stir in the flour with a wooden spoon, about 5 minutes. Be careful not to burn the flour.

Add the warm milk to the butter-flour mixture and bring to a boil, whisking constantly. Reduce the heat to medium-low and simmer for about 15 minutes until it thickens. Season with the nutmeg and salt and pepper to taste. Taste to ensure the flour flavor has gone. If you still taste the flour, cook a few minutes more.

IMPORTANTE! For a thicker besciamella, add ½ tablespoon butter and ½ tablespoon flour and cook for a few more minutes over medium-low, stirring constantly. To thin a sauce, add 1 tablespoon milk (or 2, if needed) instead.

PESTO LASAGNE

LASAGNE AL PESTO

G: *If you think lasagne is a meat-and-tomato-sauce-only dish, think again. This staple of my youth is elegant, mouthwatering, and can easily be part of a multi-course meal without filling you up. Just remember that with no-boil lasagne noodles, they won't cook properly unless each "sheet" is completely covered in sauce.*

Butter, for greasing the pan

3 cups Besciamella (page 67)

1½ (9-ounce) boxes of no-boil lasagna noodles

Pesto (page 63)

1 cup freshly grated Parmigiano-Reggiano, plus more for serving

Extra virgin olive oil, for serving

Preheat the oven to 375°F.

Butter a 9 × 13-inch baking dish. Spread a thin layer of the besciamella (about ½ cup) over the bottom of the dish. Cover with a layer of lasagne noodles, then another layer of besciamella. Gently spread 4 tablespoons of pesto across the surface, followed by 2 tablespoons Parmesan. Repeat until you reach the top, which should be a final layer of noodles and an uppermost layer of besciamella, topped with pesto and Parmesan.

Bake for about 30 minutes until bubbly and golden brown on top. For a nice crisp coating, turn on the broiler and bake for another 5 minutes. Let rest for 5 minutes before serving. Keep extra virgin olive oil and Parmesan handy for a final garnish before serving.

IMPORTANTE! On its own, pesto can oxidize and turn dark, but in a lasagne, the besciamella protects the basil, so you can keep this lasagne in the fridge for a few days and it won't turn dark. It can also be frozen after baking.

BUCATINI
ALL'AMATRICIANA

This warming, subtly piquant pasta from the village of Amatrice is a direct evolution of the Gricia (page 71) in that you're essentially just adding tomatoes to make this classic. You can give this dish a more summery feel by using heirloom cherry tomatoes cut into quarters rather than puréed canned tomatoes, but remember it should still be served hot, never cold or at room temperature.

Kosher salt and freshly ground black pepper

2 tablespoons extra virgin olive oil, plus more for serving

¼ pound guanciale or pancetta, diced

3 garlic cloves, chopped

1 teaspoon hot red pepper flakes

1 (28-ounce) can whole peeled tomatoes (pelati), puréed in a blender

6 fresh basil leaves, torn

1 pound bucatini or thick spaghetti

1 tablespoon finely chopped fresh Italian parsley

Freshly grated Parmigiano-Reggiano or aged Pecorino cheese, for serving

In an 8- to 12-quart pot, bring 6 quarts of salted water to a rolling boil.

In a large skillet, heat the olive oil over medium-high heat until hot. Add the guanciale and sauté for 5 to 7 minutes, until golden brown.

Add the garlic and red pepper flakes and sauté for 1 minute. Add the puréed tomatoes, basil, and salt and pepper to taste. Reduce the heat to medium-low and stir well. Cook, uncovered, for 15 minutes, or until the sauce darkens and thickens.

Add the pasta to the boiling water and use a wooden fork to stir the pasta so it won't stick together. Cook until al dente. Drain and add the pasta to the sauce. Increase the heat to high and toss the pasta with the sauce for 1 minute, to make sure the sauce is evenly distributed.

Serve with a sprinkling of parsley and cheese and a drizzle of olive oil.

PASTA ALLA GRICIA

G: *History tells us that Grisciano shepherds would cook this dish as they traveled from the mountains of Central Italy to Rome to sell their cheese and pigs. With the cured pig jowl known as* guanciale *hanging from their belts, they'd stop to feed themselves by slicing off bits of the guanciale and making this powerful traditional recipe. In certain ways it is the mother of two very famous meat-essential pasta sauces, the Amatriciana (page 69) and the Carbonara (page 74), and though you can be forgiven for substituting pancetta (which comes from pork belly), guanciale is the way to go. It's that much more delicious. Why else would those shepherds keep it with them at all times? I also added sage leaves to the recipe, since I think that surely a shepherd camping by a river would forage for some wild herbs to cook with it. (Well, at least I would!)*

3 tablespoons extra virgin olive oil, plus more for serving

½ pound guanciale, cut into ⅓-inch-thick strips 2 inches long

5 garlic cloves, coarsely chopped

5 fresh sage leaves

Kosher salt and freshly ground black pepper

1 pound pasta, such as penne or spaghetti

¾ cup freshly grated Pecorino cheese, plus more for serving

In a large skillet, heat the olive oil over medium-high heat until hot but not smoking. Add the guanciale and cook for about 10 minutes, making sure the meat does not get too crunchy.

Add the garlic and cook for another 2 minutes, until both the guanciale and garlic are a golden brown. (If you see the garlic browning too fast, you can always remove it from the pan and add it back in later.) Add the sage, cook for 2 minutes, and remove the sauce from the heat.

In an 8- to 12-quart pot, bring 6 quarts of salted water to a rolling boil. Add the pasta and use a wooden fork to stir the pasta so it won't stick together. Cook until al dente. Drain and add to the sauce in the pan. Toss over medium-high heat for 1 minute. Add the ¾ cup Pecorino and toss for 1 more minute.

Garnish with grated Pecorino, a drop of extra virgin olive oil, and freshly ground black pepper.

PAPPARDELLE
with duck ragu

PAPPARDELLE ALLA RAGÙ DI ANATRA

· SERVES 6 ·

Ragus that cook for hours deserve fresh pasta, so we suggest making homemade pappardelle for this classic meat sauce. Duck isn't one of the gamy birds, so even though the braising is a lengthy process, you're left with a succulent pasta dish that will connect you instantly to the world of the Tuscan hunter. Be sure to use drumsticks and thighs, though: duck breast is drier than those pieces and won't elicit as much flavor.

2 tablespoons extra virgin olive oil, plus more for serving

5 duck legs (drumsticks and thighs together)

Kosher salt and freshly ground black pepper

1 red onion, finely chopped

1 celery stalk, finely chopped

1 carrot, finely chopped

3 sprigs fresh thyme

1 garlic clove, finely chopped

1½ cups red wine

1 (28-ounce) can whole peeled tomatoes (pelati), puréed in a blender

Handmade Pappardelle (page 53) or 1 pound store-bought fresh

Finely chopped fresh Italian parsley, for garnish

Freshly grated Parmigiano-Reggiano cheese, for serving

In a large skillet or Dutch oven, heat the olive oil over medium-high heat until hot.

Season the duck with salt and pepper. Add the duck to the hot pan and cook for 10 to 11 minutes, or until golden brown and crisp. Transfer to a plate.

To the same pan, add the onion, celery, and carrot and sauté for 3 minutes, until soft. Add the thyme and garlic and sauté 1 minute more, until fragrant. Add the red wine and use a wooden spoon to scrape up the browned bits from the bottom of the pan: this will add to the flavor of the finished sauce. Cook for 2 minutes. Stir in the tomatoes and season with salt and pepper to taste. Reduce the heat to medium-low and bring to a light simmer.

Add the seared duck back to the pan and cover. Simmer gently for 1 hour 30 minutes, or until the duck is extremely tender and falling off the bone. Remove the pan from the heat.

Using tongs, carefully take the duck pieces from the ragu and place on a platter. Remove the skin and bones from the duck and discard. Chop the duck meat finely and

add back into the tomato sauce, adding ½ cup water if it looks dry. Cover and simmer over medium-low heat for 40 minutes.

In an 8- to 12-quart pot, bring 6 quarts of salted water to a rolling boil. Add the Pappardelle and use a wooden fork to stir the pasta so it won't stick together. Cook until al dente. Drain.

Serve the ragu over the pasta, drizzle with a little olive oil, and sprinkle with parsley and Parmesan.

SPAGHETTI ALLA CARBONARA

Another relative of Pasta alla Gricia's (page 71) is this Roman-born staple, which is sometimes referred to as "coal miner's spaghetti." While the word carbonara *makes obvious reference to carbon, it's also an Italian term for "charcoal burner." Imagine hungry, soot-encased miners getting a hot meal cooked over the very source they're extracting from the earth. This Gricia variation—a favorite of our kids—adds protein by way of the egg. Cream is often used in American versions. The best way to get that rich, milky texture is to let the raw egg develop into a velvety consistency when added to the cooked pasta that has been loosened with a little bit of pasta water. Also, we suggest avoiding bacon as a substitute for guanciale: bacon's smokiness would change the whole flavor profile.*

Kosher salt

3 tablespoons extra virgin olive oil, plus more for serving

¼ pound guanciale, sliced (or diced pancetta or prosciutto)

2 garlic cloves, sliced

1 pound spaghetti

1 large egg

3 large egg yolks

½ cup freshly grated Pecorino cheese

½ teaspoon freshly ground black pepper

Freshly grated Parmigiano-Reggiano, for serving

In an 8- to 12-quart pot, bring 6 quarts of salted water to a rolling boil.

Meanwhile, in a large skillet, heat the olive oil over medium-high heat. Add the guanciale and cook for 7 to 10 minutes, or until golden brown. Add the garlic and sauté for 2 minutes. Remove from the heat and transfer with the rendered fat to a ceramic bowl to cool.

Add the spaghetti to the boiling water and use a wooden fork to stir the pasta so it won't stick together. Cook until al dente. Ladle out ½ cup of the pasta water, then drain the pasta and put it in another large ceramic bowl.

In a medium bowl, whisk together the whole egg, egg yolks, Pecorino, and pepper. Whisk in the cooled guanciale. Add to the bowl of hot pasta and toss until completely mixed, adding some of the reserved pasta water for desired creaminess.

Serve immediately, sprinkled with Parmesan and a drizzle of olive oil.

IMPORTANTE! Use the best, freshest possible organic eggs, since there are raw eggs in this recipe. The best way to check the freshness is to fill a deep bowl with water, then put the eggs in one at a time. If an egg sinks right away, it's fresh—it indicates a minimum amount of air inside. If it floats, don't use it.

BAKED PASTA IN EGGPLANT

PASTA INCACIATA

· SERVES 8–12 ·

G: *This wow-factor pasta cake wrapped in eggplant is an homage to my friend Nick Stellino, a wonderful Sicilian chef, author, and TV personality Deborah and I got to know when we lived in Los Angeles. He made this for me and I loved it so much I wanted to work on my own version. My Tuscan upbringing inspired me to use a traditional Tuscan meat sauce. Also, growing up in a kosher household I came to appreciate keeping meat and dairy separate—mainly because the two together can feel very heavy. So I cut the amount of mozzarella used and left out the besciamella that acted as a binding agent. If you want that sliced-cake experience though, whisk a couple of eggs and pour that into the pasta-sauce mixture when it's in the springform pan. The eggs will cook and bind your "cake."*

Butter, softened, for greasing the pan

¼ cup plus 2 tablespoons dried bread crumbs

4 tablespoons freshly grated Parmigiano-Reggiano cheese, plus more for topping

2 tablespoons extra virgin olive oil, plus more as needed for frying

1 pound ground pork

Salt and freshly ground black pepper

2 garlic cloves, coarsely chopped

½ cup red wine, such as Chianti

4 cups Red Sauce (page 55)

1 pound ziti or penne

2 medium eggplants, cut lengthwise into ¼-inch-thick planks

1 pound fresh mozzarella cheese, shredded, plus more for sprinkling

Grease the bottom and sides of a 9-inch springform pan with softened butter. In a small bowl, combine the ¼ cup bread crumbs with 2 tablespoons of the Parmesan. Use the mixture to evenly coat the insides of the springform. Shake out whatever doesn't adhere to the butter and discard.

In a large skillet, heat 2 tablespoons of the olive oil over medium heat until hot. Add the ground pork and season with salt and pepper to taste. Sauté for about 10 minutes, or until cooked through.

Add the garlic and cook until fragrant, about 2 minutes. Stir in the red wine and simmer until reduced by half, about 5 minutes. Add the Red Sauce, bring the mixture back to a simmer, and cook for another 5 minutes to blend the flavors. Season the meat sauce with salt and pepper to taste.

(continued)

In an 8- to 12-quart pot, bring 6 quarts of salted water to a rolling boil. Add the pasta to the boiling water and use a wooden fork to stir the pasta so it won't stick together. Cook until al dente. Drain, then set aside in a large bowl.

Meanwhile, season the eggplants with salt and pepper. In a large skillet, heat 2 tablespoons olive oil over medium-high heat until hot. Add the eggplant in batches of 7 or 8 slices, cooking about 3 minutes per side, until golden brown. Replenish the pan with 2 more tablespoons of olive oil before each new batch. Drain the eggplant on a paper towel–lined baking sheet.

Add the mozzarella and sauce to the bowl with the cooked pasta.

To assemble, line the bottom of the prepared springform pan with a single layer of eggplant, then line the sides vertically with the eggplant so each "plank" hangs over the outside. Fill the inside of the pan with the pasta mixture, pressing down gently. Fold the flaps of eggplant over the top of the pasta, using any remaining eggplant slices to cover the top. Cover with plastic wrap and weight it down with a plate. Refrigerate the pan for 3 to 4 hours, or even overnight.

Preheat the oven to 350°F.

Remove the plastic and sprinkle mozzarella, the remaining 1 tablespoon Parmesan, and the remaining 2 tablespoons bread crumbs over the top. Cover loosely with foil, place the pan on a baking sheet, and bake for 30 minutes. Remove the foil and bake an additional 15 minutes, until the top is golden brown and bubbling.

Remove from the oven and let rest for 15 to 20 minutes, so it can cool slightly. Open the pan's latch and gently remove the pasta cake from the pan. Slice and serve.

FOUR-CHEESE PENNE

PENNE AI QUATTRO FORMAGGI

D: *So many of us have surrendered to boxed macaroni with powdered cheese when dealing with the growling stomachs of kids, but we say try the four-cheese Tuscan version next time! The Taleggio's smokiness, the hint of blue from the Gorgonzola, the sharpness of the Gruyère, and Parmigiano's natural saltiness—a combo straight from Gabriele's Nonna—make for a rich, fantastic combination that even parents will happily devour.*

Kosher salt and freshly ground black pepper

1 cup whole milk

¼ pound Taleggio cheese, cut into small cubes

¼ pound Gorgonzola cheese, cut into small cubes

2 ounces Gruyère cheese, grated

2 ounces freshly grated Parmigiano-Reggiano cheese, plus more for topping

1 pound mezze pasta (short penne)

⅓ cup dried bread crumbs

In an 8- to 12-quart pot, bring 6 quarts of salted water to a rolling boil.

In a large saucepan, heat the milk over medium heat for 3 to 5 minutes, or until you see steam, but before it boils. Add all of the cheeses and heat over medium heat, stirring gently but consistently with a wooden spoon, for 8 to 10 minutes, or until the cheese is melted and no lumps remain. Remove from the heat.

Add the penne to the boiling water and use a wooden fork to stir the pasta so it won't stick together. Cook until al dente. Drain, add to the sauce, and toss well. Season with salt and a generous amount of pepper.

Preheat the broiler.

Divide the penne into ten 6-ounce ramekins or a 9 × 13-inch baking dish, top with the bread crumbs, and a sprinkling of Parmesan, and place on the top rack of your oven. Bake for 3 to 5 minutes, or until the top is golden and crisp. Serve immediately.

LINGUINE AI LANGOSTINI

SERVES 6

G: *Italians don't grow up with the gargantuan lobsters that Americans do—we have the Mediterranean-friendly langostinos, which for us are like baby lobsters, or overgrown prawns. Frozen langostinos aren't that hard to find anymore in the United States, but there's nothing as satisfying as plating a whole, fresh crustacean. Try this in summer with a glass of dry white wine, and you'll have an instant kinship with diners up and down the Italian coast!*

2 tablespoons extra virgin olive oil, plus more for serving

3 garlic cloves, roughly chopped

Pinch of hot red pepper flakes, plus more for garnish

1 tablespoon finely chopped fresh Italian parsley

1½ pounds langostinos or Santa Barbara spot prawns, deveined, shells on

½ cup dry white wine

1 (28-ounce) can whole peeled tomatoes (pelati), puréed in a blender

Salt and freshly ground black pepper

1 pound linguine

1 tablespoon torn fresh basil, for garnish

In a large skillet, heat the olive oil over medium-high heat until hot. Add the garlic and red pepper flakes and sauté for 1 minute, until fragrant. Add the parsley and langostinos and cook for 3 to 5 minutes, turning them, until the color turns from dark gray (uncooked) to a vivid pink (cooked). Add the wine and stir well until you can no longer detect a sharp alcohol aroma, about 1 minute.

Transfer the langostinos to a bowl. Peel the shells off 2 of the langostinos, chop them into ½-inch pieces, and set aside.

Add the tomatoes to the sauce in the skillet, stir, season with salt and pepper to taste, and simmer over medium-low heat for about 15 minutes to meld the flavors. Add the chopped langostinos and simmer for another 3 minutes.

In an 8- to 12-quart pot, bring 6 quarts of salted water to a rolling boil. Add the linguine to the water and use a wooden fork to stir the pasta so it won't stick together. Cook until al dente. Drain, then add the cooked pasta to the sauce in the skillet. Over medium-high heat, stir the pasta in the sauce for up to 1 minute.

Serve on a platter with the remaining whole, cooked langostinos on top. Garnish with the basil, a drizzle of olive oil, and a sprinkle of red pepper flakes.

ANGRY LOBSTER PASTA

L'ARAGOSTA ARRABBIATA

G: *This is a lobster-mad dish, or more appropriately, lobster-angry, since it's paired with the "angry" pasta sauce known as* arrabbiata. *If you think only of melted butter when it comes to lobster, try this leaner, spicier red sauce version; it will satisfy you just as much. (I cooked it for Anthony Bourdain, and he had three servings of it!)*

3 (1-pound) or 2 (1½-pound) live lobsters

Sea salt and freshly ground black pepper

5 tablespoons extra virgin olive oil

4 garlic cloves, thinly sliced

1 teaspoon hot red pepper flakes

½ cup dry white wine

2 pints cherry tomatoes, halved

1 pound spaghetti

12 fresh basil leaves, torn, for garnish

Bring a 16-quart pot of water (for the lobsters) and a separate 9- to 10-quart pot with 6 quarts of salted water (for the pasta) to a boil. It's best if the lobster pot has a lid.

Place the lobsters in the boiling water head first and cover tightly with the lid. (If you have lobsters of different weights, put the heaviest lobster in first, wait 1 minute, then add the others.) Boil the lobsters for about 7 minutes, but no longer than 8 minutes—you want them to be slightly underdone. Remove the lobsters to a cutting board. Holding each lobster upside down, twist the body to separate it from its head. Set aside the heads in a bowl. Remove the lobster legs from the bodies and set aside.

In a 14-inch skillet, heat the olive oil over medium-high heat. Add the reserved lobster heads; make sure they face up so the juices collect in the pan. Include any juices that collected in the bowl. Cook for about 5 minutes, then discard the heads.

Meanwhile, crack open the claws and remove the meat. Cut open the tail to remove the tail meat. Cut all of the meat into 1- to 2-inch pieces.

To the same skillet, add the garlic and red pepper flakes and cook for 2 minutes, until fragrant. Add the wine and cook for 5 minutes, until the wine has reduced by half. Add the tomatoes and salt and pepper to taste, and cook for 3 to 5 minutes, until they just break down.

Add the spaghetti to the second pot of boiling water and cook until al dente. Ladle out 1 cup of the pasta water, then drain the pasta.

Add the lobster meat, reserved legs, and pasta to the sauce and toss together for about 1 minute, adding pasta water as needed to give more fluidity to the sauce. Serve immediately garnished with the basil.

REEF PENNETTE

PENNETTE ALLO SCOGLIO

─────── SERVES 4–6 ───────

G: *I think of this dish as a microcosm of sea flavors.* Scoglio *refers to the rock or reef around which shellfish, mussels, and small fish thrive. Although scoglio pasta is traditionally made from whatever seafood odds and ends a poor farmer or fisherman can find, you can think of this as a way to mix and match whatever catches your eye at the market.*

1 pound mussels

1 pound clams

Kosher salt and freshly ground
   black pepper

2 tablespoons extra virgin olive oil,
   plus more for serving

3 garlic cloves, roughly chopped

1 teaspoon hot red pepper flakes,
   plus more for serving

1 cup puréed canned whole peeled
   tomatoes (pelati)

1 tablespoon finely chopped fresh Italian
   parsley, plus more for garnish

1 pound pennette or spaghetti

Clean the mussels by pulling out their beards from the narrow end of the shell, away and down, toward their broadest portion. Rinse the mussels well, scrubbing them vigorously (preferably with a mussel brush) to remove impurities from the shells.

Place the mussels and clams in a large skillet, cover, and cook over medium-high heat for 1 to 2 minutes. Check to see which mussels and clams have opened and move them to a bowl. Continue cooking the unopened mussels and clams, covered, checking every minute and removing those that have opened. After a total of 5 minutes, discard any unopened mussels or clams. Transfer the released juices from the skillet to a bowl.

In an 8- to 12-quart pot, bring 6 quarts of salted water to a rolling boil.

In the same skillet, heat the olive oil over medium-high heat until hot. Add the garlic and sauté for 2 to 3 minutes, until the garlic starts to color. Add the red pepper flakes, stir well, and cook for 1 minute more. Add the tomatoes and parsley and season with salt and pepper to taste. Pour in ½ cup of the reserved seafood juices. Stir well, reduce the heat to medium, and cook for about 15 minutes until the sauce is reduced by one-third and the flavors have melded.

Add the mussels and clams to the sauce, stir well, and cook for 5 minutes.

Add the pasta to the boiling water, using a wooden fork so it won't stick together. Cook until al dente. Drain, then add the pasta to the skillet. Toss well with the sauce.

Serve with a garnish of parsley, a drizzle of olive oil, and if so desired, an extra touch of red pepper flakes.

SPAGHETTI ALLE VONGOLE

D: *There's a reason this is an Italian classic: When the clams release their wonderfully salty juice, you want that perfect welcoming party for it, and that's where the white wine, garlic, and pepper flakes come in. Sea and spice!*

Kosher salt and freshly ground
   black pepper

3 pounds Manila clams

1 pound spaghetti

3 tablespoons extra virgin olive oil,
   plus more for serving

3 garlic cloves, finely chopped

½ teaspoon hot red pepper flakes,
   plus more for serving

½ cup dry white wine

1 tablespoon finely chopped fresh Italian
   parsley, for serving

In an 8- to 12-quart pot, bring 6 quarts of salted water to a rolling boil.

Place the clams in a large skillet, cover, and heat over medium-high heat for 3 minutes. Remove the lid and transfer any opened clams to a bowl to cool. Cover the skillet again and cook for 1 to 2 minutes more. Remove the lid and again transfer any opened clams to the bowl. If after 1 more minute of cooking, there are clams that haven't opened, discard them and remove the skillet from the heat. Pour the broth released by the clams into a bowl and set aside.

Once the clams have cooled, remove the meat from three-fourths of the opened clams and chop finely. Discard the shells. If you can capture any leftover clam juice, add to the reserved broth. Set the clam meat and clams still in their shells aside.

Add the spaghetti to the boiling water and use a wooden fork to stir the pasta so it won't stick together. Cook until al dente.

In the same skillet used to cook the clams, heat the olive oil over medium-high heat until hot. Add the garlic and red pepper flakes and cook for 2 to 3 minutes, until the garlic is fragrant but not burnt. Add the wine and cook for 3 to 5 minutes more, until it's reduced by about one-third.

Add the chopped clams and the clams still in their shells to the skillet, along with ½ cup of the reserved broth. Reduce the heat to medium-low, season with salt and pepper to taste, stir the clams into the sauce, and cook for 3 to 5 minutes to coat the clams.

Drain the spaghetti and add to the sauce. Raise the heat to high and toss the cooked pasta and sauce together until the spaghetti is well coated, about 1 minute.

Serve with a drizzle of olive oil, and sprinkled with the parsley and a touch more red pepper flakes.

ON ENTERTAINING

D: The first great hostess I knew was my grandmother. She was a single woman living in a house in Queens. Until I was five years old my mother and I lived with her. She loved to set a beautiful table when people came over, and she always wore an apron over a pretty dress. She'd take off her heels, put on comfortable shoes, and get started. We had very little money but she insisted on a formal setting. She'd go out to her yard and cut hydrangeas and roses and various greens for floral arrangements. I remember the dishware as very eclectic, the cloth napkins never matched, and tablecloths couldn't be called new. But she had a sewing kit and when something wore out, she'd mend it herself, sewing a hole or adding lace trim to freshen it up.

My mother had a more relaxed approach. Formality wasn't her style: Creating a loose, fun vibe was. She wasn't a great cook, but it was hard not to be caught up in the energy of the large, communal dinners she had. The stereo would blare Frank Zappa, The Doors, or Janis Joplin, psychedelic lights might be flashing, and there were usually dancing guests. There were always children around, too.

Until I met Gabriele, these were the hostesses whose styles were most imprinted on me. From my grandmother I inherited the importance of showing your guests you care, and how a meager budget and elegant, colorful table setting aren't mutually exclusive. From my mother, I understood how that all-essential "let's have a good time" atmosphere could overcome even the least-appetizing meal. Then I met Gabriele's mother, a genius at party preparation, and my hosting horizons expanded even further: I learned how with the right organization, you can throw a perfect party, and enjoy it yourself, without feeling frantic!

Here's great advice I can give you on turning your next small dinner party, family get-together, or bells-and-whistles blowout into an opportunity to feel that special hosting pride.

PARTY SIZE

My favorite size of dinner party is six to eight adults: It's manageable, there's enough space, and conversation doesn't break off into cliques. Everybody gets to hear and participate. I'm not the kind of hostess who thinks it should be all couples, or all singles, either. We've had plenty of situations where it's mostly couples and one unattached but interesting man or woman, and nobody feels uncomfortable.

My feeling about seating arrangements is usually every-guest-for-his-or-her-self, but it's occasionally fun to put people together who you know have never met before. For us that's often turned out fabulously, and each guest ends up having the time of their lives. When I plan the seating, I encourage my daughters to design place cards, a task they love.

TABLE SETTING

At the end of the day, any home cook can offer a great table experience. When we lived in Los

Angeles, our garden was an exciting source of table ideas: ferns, leaves, eucalyptus branches, birds of paradise, and fresh flowers. Something to always remember is that whatever's gracing the center of your table should be very low. I don't like it when I have to crane my neck around the floral arrangement to see the person across from me. A small sturdy cup of water or a short vase will do the trick. Sometimes I like to float a gardenia blossom in a bowl. It opens up at the table and offers a beautiful fragrance. And if you don't have a garden, just go to a local florist or corner store and buy something inexpensive. Or skip the flowers altogether and go with low candles, always a sublimely decorative option. Then there's letting your ornamental imagination fly with well-placed tchotchkes. In our house that might translate into displaying our cute collection of miniature musical instruments, or glass fruit, or my proud collection of tiny, vintage mini-spy cameras and lady shavers! If it's a conversation starter, all the better. As for plates, the dark-colored kind look better than white once your beautifully

presented food gets cut and moved around. Remember, you're looking to make the table a happy, lively, and visually appealing place.

THRIFT STORES ARE YOUR FRIEND
I didn't have a lot of money when I moved into my first place—yet I still wanted to entertain, even though I couldn't afford to buy stuff from specialty shops or department stores. That's when I fell in love with flea markets, vintage shops, yard sales, and junk stores. Sure, the items there are not top dollar, and finding pieces that match is a lost cause, but you will still find beautiful things that have a history. A fancy dinner may be exquisitely decorated with the best wine and floral arrangements, and an overwhelming sense of matchy-matchiness, but when you go to someone's home and the vibe is of stylish, hand-picked pieces with character—a cool, unusual tablecloth, an eccentric salt-and-pepper shaker, mementos from other countries, with different wine glasses at every setting—it adds so much color and excitement. I think the personalized touch is much more important than the dining display that smacks of money, and the more you become acquainted with thrift spots, the keener your eye will become to making beautiful table design happen on a budget.

Although I prefer the personal experience of seeking and discovering that comes from haunting thrift shops and garage sales, remember that eBay is a great resource, too, for deals on dishes, glasses, and vases when you don't have time to get out.

NAPKINS
A napkin is there to serve a purpose—to protect your clothes and to keep your hands and face clean. That said, I love a cloth napkin as a way to

dress up a table. But I'm very utilitarian about it. I don't want them pressed or rolled up or stuffed into a napkin holder, and they don't all need to be the same print or color, either: just roughly the same size. I stay away from dark-colored napkins because I believe when people wipe their mouths, they want to see that the napkin's done the job. I also go with older cotton napkins, if possible, because they're often heavier and more durable and wash well. Before I use them, I always wash them in very hot water and bleach. I prefer cotton to linen because I don't have to iron them, and anything's better than synthetic, which absorbs nothing and leaves white lint on your clothes.

VASES, DECANTERS, AND PITCHERS

Over the years, I've amassed a wonderful collection of vintage vases and pitchers that sometimes get used for floral arrangements or as vessels for drinking water, depending on the mood. When it comes to wine though, I have found that the right vase can also make an interesting wine decanter. I have a couple of small ones made of terra cotta, one with red grapes on it for red and white grapes for white. This isn't for fancy wine, mind you. We have expensive decanters, too, and if the bottle is pricey and the dinner party is small and kid-free, we use those. But if you find a vase you think would make a good decanter, fill it up with very hot water and bleach, then scrub it vigorously with a baby-bottle brush. I'm telling you, vases as decanters make for great conversation pieces.

WINEGLASSES

How many times have we been at someone's house when a wineglass gets knocked over and breaks? That's why my favorite glass for drinking wine is a classic Italian trattoria glass:

solid-bottomed and small, with real weight to it. It's casually festive and doesn't make you fear you'll snap it in two in your hand. Trattoria glasses prevent excessively poured amounts, too, so people can think they're drinking more when they're really not. They're great all-purpose glasses also, whether for adults having an afternoon *caffè* or kids drinking juice. You can also buy them in bulk inexpensively at a place like Crate & Barrel or Sur La Table, which makes replacing them not a big deal.

THE IMPORTANCE OF PREPARATION

I'd thrown plenty of parties and dinners before meeting Gabriele, but one of the greatest gifts I received after falling in love with my future husband was getting to watch his mother, Annalisa, masterfully entertain. It was her sense of timing that was most impressive to me, how much she'd obviously thought out the party and prepared for it. I thought about my own festive but slapdash affairs, when I'd still be in the kitchen going crazy, never able to have as good a time as my guests. What Annalisa taught me was the importance of making a list of what has to get done and the best order. This is so that what can be done early gets done early and what can only be done at the last minute— usually cooking-related—isn't a source of hair-pulling stress. It means allowing time to get yourself showered, dressed, and ready before guests arrive, but maybe giving yourself some tasks that have to get done first. It also means knowing when something is coming out of the oven, when something can be prepared ahead, and—as strange as this may sound—when you can leave something for your first guests to help you with. I'm a big believer in the sense of community that hosting can inspire, and asking guests for help gives them the feeling that it's their party, too: dressing a salad, setting out the cutlery or plates you've chosen for the party, slicing cheeses and meats for an appetizer plate. If you've turned on some music and put a glass of wine in their hands, they're more likely to feel relaxed and less likely to want to leave you with all the final-stage work.

KIDS' PARTIES

These loom large in a parent's mind: Will it go smoothly? Will the kids be happy? Will the parents be happy? And lastly, when will they go home? On that last one, I can tell you, it's about establishing the end time right off the bat. It's not "Be here at 11:00!" It's "The party is from 11:00 to 1:30!" And emphasize the 1:30! But that means preparation and having a strong sense of what the schedule is. I like to have plenty of activities for the kids—games, a hired performer (a recommended one!), anything regimented and distracting—with one activity specifically planned for after eating so they can burn off what they've just wolfed down.

Try not to be the parent who settles for delivered pizza, potato chips, and store-bought cookies because it's easy. Our Quattro Formaggi pasta (page 79) is a real kids' party hit, a delicious alternative to boxed macaroni and cheese, served in individual ramekins so the kids have their own equal portions. Bruschetta (page 38) with mozzarella and tomatoes satisfies hungry little ones, too. We'll serve our own desserts as well, often our Schiacciata alla Fiorentina (page 239), an orangey, spongey cake on which you can make a fun stencil with the confectioners' sugar. Our Fruit Salad (page 257) is another fun choice—it's marinated in orange juice with a squeeze of lemon and can be served in parfait cups.

risotto

RISOTTI

G: I'm a musician, and when I think about the velvety, broth-cooked rice dish risotto and the way its variations showcase ingredients, it's hard not to describe the effect in performance terms. Risotto isn't the vehicle for letting an ingredient shine, the way a small trio might by way of solo riffs. It's more like an orchestra, where you as a musician become part of the whole without getting a spotlight. Bold items tend to overwhelm risotto, which is why the recipes here feature ingredients like asparagus, shrimp, zucchini, and mushrooms. They have plenty of flavor yet blend well. No wonder risotto is known to be a popular way to get children to eat vegetables—they can revel in the symphony of creaminess and rice, while the hardworking nutrient section can do its job nearly unnoticed!

When making risotto, the timing is everything. You can make a wonderful risotto, but you have to be focused. You must watch over it, stirring as you ladle in vegetable stock at specific moments. If it's overcooked, it's too mushy, and if it's undercooked, it's like gnawing on flaxseeds. Although Arborio is a popular risotto rice, I prefer Carnaroli, because it gives more of an al dente bite. I don't like soupy risottos, and the hard-to-overcook Carnaroli helps prevent that from happening. Arborio works well if you're making risotto to use in risotto croquettes, because it does give you a stickier dish, which you need to form the croquettes. Just remember that different brands of rice may require different cooking times, so be sure to check the time listed on the box you use.

You'll also notice that a few of these recipes call for a rind of Parmigiano-Reggiano cheese, typically added early in the rice-cooking process as a slow-melting seasoning. When I was growing up, we would ask at the grocery store for their rinds, and they'd sell them to us by weight. You may want to try the same, but at the very least, start saving your Parmesan rinds. (Make a lot of the recipes in this book, and you'll start collecting rinds sooner than you think!) Kept in the fridge in a resealable bag or wrapped in plastic, they'll easily last for 2 to 3 months. If you don't have a rind though, an equivalent amount in freshly grated Parmesan is about 1 tablespoon—the only difference is that you'll add that at the end, after your rice is al dente.

I also like to use as wide a pan surface as possible for risotto, no smaller than 14 inches across. That's because having the rice in one shallow layer helps the risotto cook more evenly, and it prevents soupiness. With a surface area smaller than 14 inches, the grains closer to the heat will cook sooner than the grains closer to the surface.

VEGETABLE STOCK

BRODO VEGETALE

G: *I'm a vegetable stock guy over chicken or beef stocks when it comes to risotto. I find the flavors of vegetable stock less intrusive than the meat-based kind, and more harmonious with the comforting taste I'm after. If you buy it at the store, be sure to check the sodium content: if it's heavily salted, you might need to cut it with water. The kind of stock I make doesn't use salt or pepper. I prefer to season during the cooking process. So here's all you need to whip up your own batch.*

3 carrots

3 celery stalks

1 red onion, halved

In a large stockpot, combine the carrots, celery, onion, and 8 quarts water. Bring to a boil, then reduce the heat to medium-low and simmer uncovered for 3 hours, or until reduced by one-third. Strain.

IMPORTANTE! Although these recipes generally call for 4 cups of heated vegetable stock, you might find you use less stock, or even more. That's the nature of different rice brands. Just remember that if you do need extra stock, heat it to warm before you add it. If you finish off your risotto with cold water, your rice will be soggy.

SAUSAGE AND ASPARAGUS RISOTTO

RISOTTO SALSICCIE E ASPARAGI

⊢ SERVES 4–6 ⊣

D: *We normally don't put pork in a risotto—it has a bold flavor and could overwhelm the dish. But here the sausage provides a nice, meaty texture and pairs well with asparagus, one of our favorite risotto ingredients.*

Salt and freshly ground black pepper

1 bunch thin asparagus (½ pound)

5 tablespoons extra virgin olive oil, plus more for serving

2 pork sausages (½ pound), casings removed

1 shallot, finely chopped

1 cup Carnaroli rice

½ cup dry white wine

1 (1½-ounce) piece Parmigiano-Reggiano cheese rind

1 tablespoon finely chopped fresh Italian parsley

Freshly grated Parmigiano-Reggiano, for serving

In a medium saucepan, bring 4 cups lightly salted water to a boil. Add the asparagus and cook for 5 to 7 minutes, until soft. With tongs, remove the asparagus and set aside to cool. Remove the pot from the heat and let the asparagus cooking water cool to warm.

In a deep, 14-inch nonstick sauté pan, heat 2 tablespoons of the olive oil over high heat and cook the sausage, breaking it up with a wooden spoon, until it's browned but not yet crisp. Remove the meat from the pan and set aside in a bowl to cool.

Pour the remaining 3 tablespoons olive oil into the pan, keep the heat high, and use a wooden spoon to scrape the bits of meat from the bottom. When the oil is hot, add the shallot, reduce the heat to medium-high, and sauté until softened. Add the rice to the pan and stir well for 2 to 3 minutes, until the rice begins frying. Pour in the wine, stir well, and cook for 3 to 4 minutes to let it reduce slightly.

Reduce the heat to medium-low, add the cheese rind, and slowly start adding the asparagus water, a 4- to 6-ounce ladleful at a time, stirring constantly and giving the rice time to absorb the liquid before adding another ladleful. Cook for 12 to 15 minutes until the rice is nearly al dente.

Chop the asparagus into 1-inch pieces and add them to the rice, along with the sausage meat and any juices that have collected in the bowl. Season the risotto with salt and pepper and continue cooking for 2 minutes, adding asparagus water if necessary to keep the liquid level balanced, until the water is absorbed and the rice is al dente.

Serve sprinkled with the parsley, a dash of Parmesan, and a drizzle of olive oil.

RISOTTO
with taleggio and wild carrot honey

RISOTTO TALEGGIO E MIELE DI CAROTA SELVATICA

· SERVES 4–6 ·

G: *The inspiration for this risotto was a nomadic beekeeper I met in Italy, who moves across the peninsula seasonally—a bee shepherd. His fantastic honeys are tied to the seasons. His wild carrot honey was one of my favorites, and combined with the melted Taleggio it was a wonderful discovery. If you can't find wild carrot honey, sunflower or any meadow flower honey works nicely. I wouldn't use a tree honey like pine though, because they tend to be more aggressive and bitter in flavor. You want a dollop of sweetness here, the way a drizzle of olive oil finishes a dish, not something that turns your risotto into a syrupy soup.*

4 cups vegetable stock, homemade (page 94) or store-bought

2 tablespoons extra virgin olive oil

1 tablespoon unsalted butter

1 shallot, finely diced

1 cup Carnaroli rice

½ cup dry white wine

¼ pound Taleggio or La Tur cheese, cut into ½-inch cubes

2 tablespoons freshly grated Parmigiano-Reggiano cheese, plus more for serving

Salt and freshly ground black pepper

½ head Treviso radicchio, thinly sliced

1 tablespoon finely chopped fresh Italian parsley

4 to 6 teaspoons wild carrot honey or sunflower honey

In a small pot, heat the stock over medium-low heat until just before boiling. Reduce the heat to low and keep warm.

In a deep, 14-inch nonstick sauté pan, heat the olive oil and butter over medium-high heat. Add the shallot and sauté for 2 to 3 minutes, until the shallot is softened but not colored. Add the rice and stir well, making sure to coat all the grains in oil. Toss the rice a few times, then add the wine and let it reduce for 2 to 3 minutes.

Reduce the heat to medium-low and slowly start adding the stock, a 4- to 6-ounce ladleful at a time. Stir constantly, giving the rice time to absorb the liquid each time before adding another ladleful, until the rice is al dente, 15 to 25 minutes.

Add the Taleggio and let it melt completely, about 4 minutes. Add the Parmesan and season with salt and pepper to taste. Remove the pan from the heat and add the radicchio, stirring to mix it well with the rice.

Serve on plates garnished with the parsley, a touch of grated Parmesan, and lastly, a generous teaspoon of the honey.

SHRIMP AND ZUCCHINI RISOTTO

RISOTTO ZUCCHINI E GAMBRETTI

This seafood/vegetable risotto is a staple in Italy's coastal areas. Cooking the zucchini separately from the risotto is necessary for the uniformity of the dish, otherwise it would get too soft. This way, the zucchini shares some textural consistency with the shrimp when they're added together at the end. A tip about cooking zucchini: Avoid stirring when in the pan, because they'll break too easily. Toss the pan with a sharp whip of the wrist to move the zucchini around.

4 cups vegetable stock, homemade (page 94) or store-bought

3 tablespoons extra virgin olive oil, plus more for serving

5 small zucchini, cubed

2 tablespoons unsalted butter

2 shallots, finely chopped

1 cup Carnaroli rice

1¼ cups dry white wine

¾ pound shrimp, peeled and deveined

Kosher salt and freshly ground black pepper

1 tablespoon finely chopped fresh Italian parsley, plus more for garnish

2 tablespoons freshly grated Parmigiano-Reggiano cheese, plus more for serving

In a small pot, heat the stock over medium-low heat until just before boiling. Reduce the heat to low and keep warm.

In a deep, 14-inch nonstick sauté pan, heat 1 tablespoon of the olive oil over medium-high heat until hot. Add the zucchini and cook for about 15 minutes, until browned. Transfer the zucchini to a bowl and set aside.

In the same pan, heat 1 tablespoon of the olive oil and 1 tablespoon of the butter over medium-high heat until the butter is melted and foamy. Add the shallots and sauté for about 3 minutes, until tender.

Add the rice and stir well, making sure all grains of rice are coated. Stir in 1 cup of the wine, reduce the heat to medium-low, and cook it about 3 minutes to reduce slightly.

Reduce the heat to medium-low and slowly start adding the stock, a 4- to 6-ounce ladleful at a time, stirring constantly, giving the rice time to absorb the liquid each time before adding another ladleful, until the rice is al dente, 15 to 25 minutes.

Meanwhile, in a medium skillet, heat 1 tablespoon of the olive oil and the remaining 1 tablespoon butter over medium-high heat until the butter is melted. Add the shrimp, season with salt and pepper to taste, then add the parsley and the remaining ¼ cup wine. Reduce the heat to medium and cook for about 3 minutes, until the shrimp turns bright pink. Remove the shrimp from the pan and reserve the pan juices.

Add the Parmesan, zucchini, and cooked shrimp to the rice and stir well. Add the juices from the shrimp pan and cook for 5 minutes, until the shrimp juices are absorbed, adding stock as necessary to prevent the risotto from drying out.

Serve on plates sprinkled with parsley, Parmesan, and a drizzle of olive oil.

RISOTTO
with melon and speck

RISOTTO MELONE E SPECK

— SERVES 4–6 —

G: *Deborah makes fun of me for this risotto because she thinks it's about forcing my love of melon and cured meats onto anything. That may be true, but this also grew out of our time living in Los Angeles, where melon is available all year long. Sweet, cold cantaloupe in a warm rice dish? That might raise eyebrows back home, where this dish bucks tradition, but I found this combination a delicious match. And if you're feeling creative with the presentation, serve the risotto in the melon's half-shell!*

4 cups vegetable stock, homemade (page 94) or store-bought

1 tablespoon extra virgin olive oil, plus more for serving

2 tablespoons unsalted butter

1 shallot, finely chopped

1 cup Carnaroli rice

½ cup dry white wine

1 (1½-ounce) piece Parmigiano-Reggiano cheese rind

2 tablespoons freshly grated Parmigiano-Reggiano cheese

Sea salt and freshly ground black pepper

¼ Tuscan melon or cantaloupe, peeled and cut into ¼-inch dice (about 1 cup)

3 ounces hand-cut speck (as opposed to machine-cut), sliced into 1-inch-long, ¼-inch-thick strips

4 to 6 zucchini flowers (optional; for garnish)

In a small pot, heat the stock over medium-low heat until just before boiling. Reduce the heat to low and keep warm.

In a deep 14-inch nonstick sauté pan, heat the olive oil and 1 tablespoon of the butter over medium-high heat until the butter melts. Add the shallot and sauté for 4 to 5 minutes, until softened but not colored. Add the rice and stir well, evenly coating all the grains. Add the wine and cook for 2 to 3 minutes to let it reduce. Add the cheese rind and season with pepper to taste. Reduce the heat to medium-low and slowly start adding the stock, a 4- to 6-ounce ladleful at a time. Stir constantly and give the rice time to absorb the liquid each time before adding another ladleful, until the rice is al dente, 15 to 25 minutes.

Remove the rice from the heat and season with sea salt to taste. Stir in the remaining 1 tablespoon butter and the grated Parmesan. Set aside to cool for 5 to 7 minutes, until the risotto is room temperature. Add the melon and speck, stir well, and serve immediately on plates with a drizzle of olive oil and a zucchini flower.

RISOTTO
with squab and mushrooms

RISOTTO PICCIONE E FUNGHI

SERVES 4–6

G: *Pigeon meat is leaner than that of a lot of birds we eat, so it has a bit more bite to it, but it's also incredibly satisfying. It goes really well with the porcini mushrooms and the minty Italian herb called* nipitella, *creating a cold season classic, and a real favorite with hunters in my homeland.*

½ pound fresh porcini mushrooms, cleaned and cut into ¼-inch-thick strips, or 2 ounces dried porcini

4 cups vegetable stock, homemade (page 94) or store-bought

3 tablespoons extra virgin olive oil, plus more for serving

2 squab breasts (5 ounces each) or guinea fowl breasts

5 fresh sage leaves

1 garlic clove

1 sprig fresh nipitella or 2 small sprigs thyme and mint

Salt and freshly ground black pepper

2 tablespoons unsalted butter

1 shallot, finely chopped

1 cup Carnaroli rice

½ cup dry white wine

1 (1½-ounce) piece Parmigiano-Reggiano cheese rind or ¼ cup freshly grated Parmigiano-Reggiano cheese, plus more for serving

Chopped fresh Italian parsley, for garnish

If working with dried porcini, soak the mushrooms in lukewarm water for about 20 minutes.

In a small pot, heat the stock over medium-low heat until just before boiling. Reduce the heat to low and keep warm.

In a small nonstick skillet, heat 2 tablespoons of the olive oil over medium-high heat until hot. Add the squab and sage and sear the squab, 3 minutes per side. Add a ladleful of stock, bring to a simmer, reduce the heat to medium-low, and cook for 15 minutes, until the meat is tender. Remove the meat from the pan and allow to cool. Debone the squab breast and shred the meat with your hands.

In a deep 14-inch nonstick sauté pan, heat the remaining 1 tablespoon olive oil over medium-high heat until hot. Add the garlic and sauté for 1 minute. Add the mushrooms and nipitella, season with salt and pepper to taste, then reduce the heat to medium and cook for 5 to 7 minutes until the mushrooms are soft, stirring delicately so the mushrooms don't break. Remove the mushrooms and set aside. Discard the nipitella and garlic.

To the same pan the mushrooms were in, add the butter and shallot and sauté over medium-high heat for 2 to 3 minutes, until the shallot is softened. Add the rice and stir for 2 minutes. Add the wine and cook, stirring constantly, for about 3 minutes to let it reduce. Add the cheese rind (if you're using grated Parmesan, that won't be added until later), reduce the heat to medium-low, and slowly start adding stock, a 4- to 6-ounce ladleful at a time, stirring constantly and giving the rice time to absorb the liquid before adding another ladleful, until the rice is al dente, 15 to 25 minutes.

Add the chopped squab meat and cooked porcini mushrooms, season with salt and pepper to taste, stir well, and cook for 2 to 3 minutes, adding more stock if necessary to prevent the risotto from drying out. (If using grated Parmesan instead of a cheese rind, add it in the final minutes.)

Serve on plates sprinkled with some Parmesan and parsley, and drizzled with a little olive oil.

soups

ZUPPE

G: When I think about soup, I remember my Nonna during the winter, offering a mug of hot, warming *brodo* (broth) before every meal. It was simple, earthy, and flavorful, and it got my insides ready for the hot food to come. But I also remember soup as a sneaky way that my parents got me to eat vegetables. It's a technique I was well aware of as I gulped down each bowlful, and as a dad myself now, I wholeheartedly champion it!

D: I buy every old wives' tale about soup's medicinal properties. But I also love going to the farmers' market and getting inspired by what's in season there. You can load up on fresh vegetables, go home, let those ingredients lead you in a certain direction, and before you know it you've made enough soup to last several days. It means you can feed your family for longer than just one sitting.

G: These are a handful of reliably delicious recipes that range from old-school traditional Tuscan—hot, thick, hearty, and peasant in origin—to the more sophisticated kind my wife has managed to convince me are just as delicious. You can now count me as a fan of cold cucumber soup, thanks to Deborah.

D: As my husband has come to learn, cold soups aren't just for actresses getting spa treatments. They can be so refreshing on a hot summer day.

G: Exactly. So as you enjoy these recipes, above all, let them stir in you the desire to create your own tradition in a pot.

LENTIL SOUP

ZUPPA DI LENTICCHIE

D: *This is our New Year's Eve staple, the one that provides the first bite that ensures good luck for January and beyond. Lentils have always been one of the most satisfying soup textures, and our soup version starts with a* soffritto *that gives it the loveliest pork-infused flavor.*

2 tablespoons extra virgin olive oil, plus more for serving

2 ounces pancetta or prosciutto, diced

½ red onion, finely chopped

3 celery stalks, finely chopped

2 carrots, finely chopped

1 tablespoon tomato paste

Pinch of hot red pepper flakes (optional)

1 pound dried lentils

1 (1½-ounce) piece Parmigiano-Reggiano cheese rind

Feshly grated Parmigiano-Reggiano cheese, for serving

1 tablespoon finely chopped fresh Italian parsley

Salt and freshly ground black pepper

6 to 8 slices toasted bread

In a large, heavy-bottomed pot, heat the olive oil over medium-high heat until hot. Add the pancetta (or prosciutto) and sauté for 5 minutes, or until golden but not too crisp. Add the red onion, celery, and carrots, stir well, and cook for 5 to 7 minutes, until softened. Add the tomato paste and pepper flakes (if using) and stir well with a wooden spoon.

Pour the lentils into the pot, add the cheese rind and parsley, season with salt and pepper to taste, cover with 6 cups water, and bring to a boil. Reduce the heat to medium-low and cook for about 50 minutes, stirring every 10 minutes, until the lentils are swollen, on the softer side of al dente.

Garnish with Parmesan, a drizzle of olive oil, and a slice of toasted bread on the side.

PASTA AND BEAN SOUP

PASTA E FAGIOLI

D: *We believe that two touches make this classic extra special. The first is saving some whole, unpuréed beans to put in at the end as a nice serving visual. The second is adding the pasta to each bowl individually—this way your kids, if they're pasta lovers, can be given more if they want, and your al dente pasta stays that way a little longer rather than cooking longer in the pot.*

1 pound dried red kidney beans, soaked overnight in cold water to cover

2 tablespoons extra virgin olive oil, plus more for drizzling

3 ounces guanciale, diced

3 garlic cloves

2 tablespoons fresh rosemary

1 cup canned whole peeled tomatoes (pelati), broken up

Salt and freshly ground black pepper

8 ounces ditalini or pennette

In a large heavy-bottomed pot, bring 8 cups of water to a boil. Drain the beans, add them to the boiling water, stir well, and cook for about 40 minutes until tender.

In a 12-inch nonstick skillet, heat the olive oil over medium-high heat until hot. Add the guanciale and cook for 8 to 10 minutes, until crisp. Add the garlic and rosemary and sauté for 2 minutes. Add the tomatoes and cook for 5 to 8 minutes, until the sauce starts thickening.

When the beans are ready, drain and set aside 1 cup. Transfer the rest of the beans and their cooking liquid to a blender. Purée the beans in the blender, and add them to the pot with the tomato sauce. Season with salt and pepper to taste, reduce the heat to medium, and simmer for 20 minutes, stirring every 5 minutes, to blend the flavors. Add water if needed to thin out the soup.

Meanwhile, bring a large pot of salted water to a boil. Add the pasta and cook until al dente. Drain and rinse the pasta briefly under cold water, then transfer to a large bowl. Add a drizzle of olive oil and stir well.

When the soup is ready, serve it in individual bowls. Add ½ cup pasta to each bowl and a sprinkling of the reserved whole beans. Season with pepper and top with a drizzle of olive oil.

IMPORTANTE! Although this recipe calls for guanciale, vegetarians and those keeping kosher need only leave that part of the recipe out.

TUSCAN BREAD AND VEGETABLE SOUP

RIBOLLITA

G: *All hail the Tuscan peasant farmer! He's saved up his stale bread and cheap vegetables during the winter for this very dish, a hearty, thick soup that will keep the family fed for days. Ribollita means "reboiled," and ideally you'd make your ribollita the night before, stick it in the fridge, and reheat it the next day, as it gets better while it sits. It's a cold-climate classic straight from the people of my region, and nothing put a bigger smile on my face than when my daughter Giulia, at six months, took to it as her first solid food!*

8 ounces dried cannellini beans, soaked overnight in cold water to cover

Salt and freshly ground black pepper

3 tablespoons extra virgin olive oil, plus more for serving

1 carrot, roughly chopped

½ white onion, roughly chopped

½ celery stalk, roughly chopped

2 russet (baking) potatoes, peeled and diced into ½-inch pieces

1 bunch Tuscan kale (aka lacinato, black kale, cavolo nero), leaves, stems removed, roughly chopped

½ head savoy cabbage, roughly chopped

1 (15-ounce) can whole peeled tomatoes (pelati)

½ pound stale Pane Toscano (page 216), or store-bought country bread, cut into ½-inch slices

Rinse and drain the soaked beans. Bring a medium-sized, heavy-bottomed pot full of water to a boil. Add the beans, making sure they're covered by a few inches of water, and reduce the heat to medium-high. Cook for at least 1 hour, salting the water after 40 minutes, until tender. Drain the beans and set aside.

In an 8-quart pot, heat the olive oil over medium-high heat until hot. Add the carrot, onion, and celery and sauté for 8 to 10 minutes, or until soft and translucent but not golden. Add the potatoes, kale, and cabbage and sauté for about 5 minutes, until the cabbage is wilted.

Add the tomatoes, breaking them up with a wooden spoon. Add enough water to cover the ingredients, bring to a boil, then reduce the heat to medium-low. Season with salt and pepper to taste and simmer for 1 hour 30 minutes, until it thickens considerably.

Add the bread and continue cooking for another 30 minutes, until the crust of the bread begins falling apart.

Serve in bowls with an extra drizzle of olive oil.

IMPORTANTE! If you're short on time, or don't feel like soaking dried beans over-night, use 1 (15-ounce) can of cannellini beans. Rinse them, and add them to the pot later in the cooking process when the soup is thickening. Canned beans are already pretty buttery, so they don't need to be cooked an extra hour or they'll turn into paste. Also, I suggest you don't serve this soup with grated cheese. It takes away from the flavor of the fresh vegetables. To reheat ribollita, keep the heat low and reheat slowly so as not to scorch the bottom of the pot and disrupt the flavors. Add water if needed, because the bread will have absorbed the juices overnight and the soup will thicken.

TUSCAN BREAD AND TOMATO SOUP

PAPPA AL POMODORO

D: *Much like the Ribollita (page 110) was for our youngest daughter, this richly textured tomato-bread bowl of goodness was an early solid food hit with our first child, Evelina, after Gabriele's mother made it for us on a visit to Tuscany. As soon as we got back to the States, we started hoarding stale bread as if we were farmers! You could have knocked someone out with the bag of crusty pieces that kept growing in the corner of our kitchen. But that's how Tuscans like their thick rustic soups, with plenty of hearty, tomato-soaked chunks.*

2 tablespoons extra virgin olive oil, plus more for serving

3 garlic cloves, halved

1 (28-ounce) can whole peeled tomatoes (pelati), broken up

4 handfuls fresh whole basil leaves, plus more for garnish

Kosher salt and freshly ground black pepper

2 cups vegetable stock, homemade (page 94)

12 ounces stale Pane Toscano (page 216), or store-bought country bread, cut into ½-inch slices

In a large heavy-bottomed pot, heat the olive oil over medium-high heat until hot. Add the garlic and sauté 1 to 2 minutes, until fragrant but not browned. Add the tomatoes and basil, season with salt and pepper to taste, reduce the heat to medium, and cook for about 15 minutes, until the sauce has thickened. Add the stock, stir well, and bring to a soft boil.

Add the bread and cook for 10 minutes, stirring often. Remove the pot from the heat and let sit for 1 hour, until the bread has absorbed as much of the sauce as possible.

Stir with a wooden spoon, making sure to break down the biggest chunks of bread into smaller pieces. Return the pot to a low heat and simmer about 20 minutes, until warm, but not hot. Serve garnished with basil and a drizzle of olive oil.

MINESTRONE

G: *This Italian vegetable-soup classic is really just an excuse to go to your farmers' market and use what's in season—the time of year typically dictates what goes in the minestrone. This can be an opportunity to try vegetables you may not be accustomed to cooking. It's also great for vegetables that have begun wilting—it gives them an extra week of life in your fridge. And if you have kids who might balk at so obviously a nutrition-heavy soup, you can always throw in some cheese-filled tortellini or chunks of bread as a distraction!*

5 tablespoons extra virgin olive oil, plus more for serving

½ red onion, roughly chopped

2 carrots, roughly chopped

3 celery stalks, roughly chopped

½ teaspoon hot red pepper flakes

1 tablespoon finely chopped fresh Italian parsley

2 Roma or plum tomatoes, quartered

Salt and freshly ground black pepper

1 (1½-ounce) piece Parmigiano-Reggiano cheese rind

Freshly grated Parmigiano-Reggiano cheese, for serving

½ pound broccoli florets

⅓ cup halved green beans, ends trimmed

2 medium zucchini, cut into 1-inch chunks

2 large Yukon Gold potatoes, peeled and cut into 1-inch cubes

1 bunch Swiss chard, ripped by hand into 2-inch pieces

1 bunch whole Tuscan kale (aka lacinato, black kale, cavolo nero) leaves, stems removed

1 (15-ounce) can cannellini beans, drained and rinsed

In a large heavy-bottomed pot, heat the olive oil over medium-high heat until hot. Add the onion, carrots, and celery and sauté for 10 minutes, until soft but not browned. Add the red pepper flakes, parsley, and tomatoes and cook for 5 minutes, to blend the flavors and break down the tomatoes. (You can discard the tomato peels if you'd like.)

Add 6 cups water, season with salt and pepper to taste, then add the cheese rind, broccoli, green beans, zucchini, potatoes, chard, kale, and cannellini beans. Stir well. Bring the soup to a boil, then reduce the heat to medium-low and simmer for 50 minutes, until the vegetables have softened and the broth has thickened, or until the potatoes can be broken apart easily with a wooden spoon. Stir occasionally to make sure the vegetables break down and stay submerged in the broth. Add ½ cup water if needed to help the cooking process.

Season with salt and pepper and serve in bowls with a sprinkle of Parmesan and a drizzle of olive oil.

TUNA AND SWORDFISH SOUP

ZUPPA DI TONNO E PESCE SPADA

· SERVES 8 ·

G: *When I had the good fortune to trail the masterful Gino Angelini around his Angelini Osteria kitchen in Los Angeles, I quickly focused on this delicious amuse bouche served there. The first time I tried it, I got goose bumps—I instantly felt like a kid again, vacationing with my parents in Sardinia or Sicily. So my goal became to turn it into a full-on soup entree. The fish pieces really add to the roundness and help make it a meal.*

3 tablespoons extra virgin olive oil, plus more for serving

1 yellow onion, finely chopped

2 carrots, finely chopped

2 celery stalks, finely chopped

5 ounces cherry tomatoes or 1 tablespoon tomato paste

6 cups vegetable stock, homemade (page 94)

½ pound tuna steak, cut into ½-inch cubes

½ pound swordfish steak, cut into ½-inch cubes

½ pound cod fillet, cut into ½-inch cubes

Finely chopped fresh Italian parsley, for garnish

Toasted bread, for serving

In a large heavy-bottomed pot, heat the olive oil over medium-high heat until hot. Add the onion, carrots, and celery and sauté for 5 to 7 minutes, until they're soft and translucent, but not golden.

Add the tomatoes and cook for 3 to 5 minutes, until the tomatoes are dissolved. (If using tomato paste, stir it in just to make sure it's evenly mixed.)

Add the stock, bring the soup to a soft boil, then reduce the heat to medium-low and simmer for about 45 minutes.

Add the tuna, swordfish, and cod and cook for 10 minutes until just cooked through.

Serve with a sprinkle of parsley, a touch of olive oil, and with toasted bread.

COLD VEGETABLE SOUP
with mint

ZUPPA FREDDA DI VERDURA E ODORE MENTA

・ SERVES 4–6 ・

D: *This is a vegetable-stock-and-dairy-based version of a chilled greens soup, which takes advantage of mint for a unique herb-y freshness to go with the butter lettuce and arugula. Gabriele developed this as a lunch soup that would be satisfyingly smooth but not warm. On a summer day when you want something cooling, it's a deliciously light, flavorful treat.*

1 tablespoon unsalted butter

1 tablespoon extra virgin olive oil

1 shallot, chopped

1 head butter lettuce, separated into leaves

3 handfuls baby arugula

4 cups vegetable stock, homemade (page 94)

Leaves from 3 sprigs fresh mint

¼ cup heavy cream

Kosher salt and freshly ground black pepper

Juice of ½ lemon (optional)

Toasted bread rubbed with garlic, for serving

In a large saucepan, heat the butter and olive oil over medium-high heat until hot. Add the shallot and cook for 4 minutes, until soft. Add the butter lettuce and arugula and stir until just soft. Add the stock and reduce the heat to medium-low and simmer for 5 minutes to blend the flavors, then remove from the heat and let cool.

Transfer the cooled soup to a blender. Add the mint leaves and blend until smooth. Add the cream and blend further to mix. Season with salt and pepper to taste.

Refrigerate for 2 hours to chill. Serve chilled with a splash of lemon juice, if desired, and with garlic toasts.

LOBSTER AND CANNELLINI BEAN SOUP

ZUPPA DI CANNELLINI E ARAGOSTA

⊢ SERVES 6 ⊣

G: *This super-Tuscan take on the American mainstay lobster was about simplifying the richness of this ordinarily butter-drenched shellfish and marrying it with the humble creaminess of my people's beloved cannellini beans. When I created this as an appetizer during my stint at the Montauk Yacht Club, diners who tasted it wanted more!*

Kosher salt and freshly ground
   black pepper

1 (2-pound) live lobster

2 tablespoons extra virgin olive oil

1 shallot, finely chopped

Pinch of hot red pepper flakes

4 cups fish stock

2 (15-ounce) cans cannellini beans,
   drained and rinsed

1 handful fresh Italian parsley, finely
   chopped

Bring an 8-quart stockpot of salted water to a boil. Add the lobster, head first, and cover tightly with a lid. Boil for 12 to 15 minutes, until the lobster is very bright red.

Using tongs, remove the lobster from the boiling water and set it aside to cool. Once cool enough to handle, crack open the claws, body, and tail and remove the meat. Reserve any juices in a bowl for adding to the soup later. Chop the lobster meat into chunks.

In a large saucepan, heat the olive oil over medium-high heat until hot. Add the shallot and sauté for 3 minutes, or until tender. Add the red pepper flakes and cook for 1 minute. Add the stock and beans, bring to a soft boil, then reduce the heat to medium-low.

Using an immersion blender, purée the beans until smooth. Add the lobster meat and the reserved juices and simmer for 5 minutes to blend the flavors.

Season with salt and pepper to taste, add the parsley, and serve.

SPICY MUSSEL SOUP
with grilled bread

COZZE ALLA TARANTINA CON FETTUNTA

SERVES 4–6

G: *When I was in the army and stationed in Florence, home comforts weren't very far away. When I could leave the base, I would zip to our house in Fiesole, eat a home-cooked meal, and be back by curfew. I would often bring a roommate, and a guy from Taranto who especially loved this mussel soup from his region, Apulia. He always wanted it super spicy. It's a dish that really reflects the simplicity and freshness of the ingredients—Deborah says it's what turned her on to enjoying mussels. With a nice chunk of garlic-rubbed, olive oil–soaked, grilled bread called* fettunta, *and a glass of chilled white wine, this is a wonderful summer meal.*

SOUP

2 tablespoons extra virgin olive oil, plus more for serving

3 garlic cloves, cut into chunks

1 teaspoon hot red pepper flakes

Salt and freshly ground black pepper

¾ pound cherry tomatoes, quartered

¾ cup dry white wine

3 pounds mussels, scrubbed and debearded

2 tablespoons finely chopped fresh Italian parsley

GRILLED BREAD (FETTUNTA)

1 loaf country bread or Pane Toscano (page 216), thickly sliced

1 garlic clove, halved

Extra virgin olive oil, for drizzling

To make the soup: In a large Dutch oven, heat the olive oil over medium-high heat until hot. Add the garlic and red pepper flakes and stir for 2 to 3 minutes, until fragrant. Season with salt and black pepper to taste. Stir in the tomatoes and cook for 5 minutes, or until you smell their sweetness. Stir in the white wine and cook for about 1 minute, until it begins to simmer. Add the mussels and cover tightly. Cook for 6 to 8 minutes, until the mussels just begin to open. Remove from the heat and discard any mussels that did not open.

Transfer to bowls, sprinkle with parsley, and drizzle with oil. Serve with the *fettunta.*

Meanwhile, **to make the grilled bread:** Preheat the broiler, or place a stovetop toaster (page 17) over high heat. Place the sliced bread on the broiler pan 4 inches from the heat (or on the stovetop toaster, if using) and grill about 1 minute per side until golden brown. Rub the garlic on both sides. Remove from the heat and drizzle generously with olive oil. Serve immediately.

salads

INSALATE

D: Gabriele and I have different histories when it comes to salads. My mom harvested so many vegetables when we lived in upstate New York. Then I lived the actress life, eating healthy with an eye toward my figure. Lettuce, fresh herbs, a few slices of fruit, a splash of oil and vinegar or lemon, and I'd be happy. Gabriele's memories of salad on the other hand, are of his mom and dad forcing him to eat it, which goes to prove that just because you're raised on a property teeming with wild leaves from a garden—arugula, radicchio, dandelion greens—not to mention all kinds of vegetables, it doesn't mean you're predisposed to like greens.

When Gabriele and I met, he saw how stocked my very-California refrigerator was with salad ingredients, and I'll admit that at first it alarmed him. (I'll never forget the face he made when he spotted alfalfa sprouts.) But he came around to the pleasures of salad, how the right melding of flavors—sweet with savory, bitter with creamy, crunchy with juicy—could be just as exciting as his beloved Tuscan meat fests. Now when we're back in Italy, we walk the grounds of our home with the kids and make family time to forage for delicious greens, vegetables, and herbs for salads. Gabriele and I experimented together with the unique bounty of each season, and these recipes are the results. They are meant to accompany a main course, and in some cases act as light, fresh entrees on their own. Since many Italian restaurants treat salad as a modest leafy side bowl—maybe with a few sliced tomatoes—this chapter very much reflects the American influence on our home eating.

A word about dressing: Avoid the bottled kind. If you have extra virgin olive oil, an assortment of vinegars, citruses, shallots, and salt and pepper, you have the ingredients for a much healthier, more delicious complement to your salad than any over-emulsified, gluey, preservative-laden bottle can offer. Once you get used to making your own dressing—whether it's adding lemon juice and seasoning directly onto the platter, or whipping up one of our vinaigrettes or your own—you'll never go back!

BUTTER LETTUCE AND POMEGRANATE SEED SALAD

LATTUGA E SEMI DI MELAGRANA

SERVES 6

D: *This salad always looks beautiful when care is given to its presentation: The supple butter lettuce and its petal-like visual, decorated with the tiny greens called* mâche—*or "lamb's lettuce"—can make any plate look like a garden has just sprung up. With the slight edge in flavor from the shallot-infused vinaigrette, and the tang from the pomegranate seeds, this salad's a real winner.*

VINAIGRETTE

1 small shallot, finely chopped

3 tablespoons champagne vinegar

⅓ cup extra virgin olive oil

**Kosher salt and freshly ground
    black pepper**

SALAD

2 small heads butter lettuce

4 ounces mâche greens

¼ cup pomegranate seeds

To make the vinaigrette: In a small bowl, combine the shallot and vinegar. Add the olive oil, whisking slowly to emulsify the mixture. Season with salt and pepper to taste.

To make the salad: Arrange the butter lettuce on a plate. Sprinkle the mâche on top.

Just before serving, dress the greens with the vinaigrette and garnish with the pomegranate seeds.

IMPORTANTE! Dried cranberries make a fine substitute for pomegranate seeds.

PEACH AND FENNEL SALAD

INSALATE DI PESCHE E FINOCCHIO

— SERVES 4–6 —

D: *Peaches add a wonderfully juicy dimension to any salad. They're sweet enough to be an ingredient but not overpowering enough to make you feel you're just eating fruit. Combined with the licorice-like essence of fennel and the saltiness of the bresaola, which is a delicious cured beef, you have a lively summer salad with succulence and depth.*

½ medium bulb fennel

¼ small red onion

3 yellow peaches, cut into thin wedges

Extra virgin olive oil, for drizzling

Juice of 1 lemon

Kosher salt and freshly ground
  black pepper

¼ pound thinly sliced bresaola

4 big handfuls wild arugula

Using a mandoline, slice the fennel and red onion thinly.

In a medium bowl, combine the fennel, red onion, and peaches. Drizzle with olive oil and the lemon juice, then sprinkle with salt and pepper to taste. Toss the mixture with your hands.

Arrange the bresaola slices around the outside of a serving platter. Arrange the arugula in the center, then place the peach mixture on top. Add another drizzle of olive oil.

IMPORTANTE! Be sure to serve this salad immediately after plating. It can't sit too long or the lemon juice will "cook" the bresaola.

BLOOD ORANGE SALAD

INSALATA SICILIANA

G: *We made this for actor Joe Mantegna and his wife one night as part of a unique themed dinner. Joe is of Sicilian heritage, and I wanted to help channel flavor memories for him of the food that comes from his homeland. This zestful Sicilian specialty that mixes oranges, fennel, and olives was a nostalgic hit for Joe. At one point, Joe even teared up. Nothing feels better than going that extra mile to make a guest feel special.*

3 blood oranges, peeled and sliced
    into thin rings

¼ red onion, very thinly sliced

1 bulb fennel, thinly sliced

4 cups baby arugula

¼ cup oil-cured olives, pitted and
    roughly chopped

¼ cup extra virgin olive oil

Juice of 1 lemon

Kosher salt and freshly ground
    black pepper

In a large bowl, combine the oranges, red onion, and fennel slices. Add the arugula and olives and toss lightly.

Just before serving, add the olive oil and lemon juice and toss. Season with salt and pepper to taste, and serve on individual plates.

SMOKED SALMON TROUT AND CUCUMBER SALAD

INSALATA DI TROTA AFFUMICATA E CETRIOLO

SERVES 4–6

D: *This makes for a really nice light lunch. The smokiness of the fish marries beautifully with the olive oil, lemon, and shallot. It's a wonderfully round flavor, full of character but not too aggressive.*

1 large head butter lettuce, torn

2 heirloom tomatoes, diced

1 English cucumber, peeled, seeded, and diced

1 teaspoon chopped fresh mint

6 fresh basil leaves, torn by hand

1 shallot, finely diced

⅓ cup extra virgin olive oil

Grated zest and juice of 1 lemon

Kosher salt and freshly ground black pepper

4 to 6 smoked salmon trout fillets, cut into 1-inch pieces

In a large bowl, combine the lettuce, tomatoes, and cucumber.

In a small bowl, combine the mint, basil, shallot, olive oil, lemon zest and juice, and salt and pepper to taste. Whisk together. Toss with the salad.

Divide the salad among individual bowls, adding fish pieces to each bowl.

GRILLED SQUID
with arugula and grapefruit vinaigrette

CALAMARI GRIGLIATI E RUCOLA

SERVES 4–6

This is a blend of char and tartness that really wakes up the palate. Between the calamari and the arugula, there's so much flavor already before the grapefruit kicks in. We use skewers when grilling the calamari because it helps keep them from falling through the grill. Either bamboo skewers soaked for 30 minutes or metal skewers work just fine.

SALAD

Grated zest of 1 lemon plus the juice of ½ lemon

¼ cup extra virgin olive oil

1 garlic clove, finely chopped

Pinch of hot red pepper flakes

⅓ cup chopped fresh Italian parsley

1 pound calamari, cleaned, tentacles removed, and bodies sliced into 1-inch rings

1 pink grapefruit

Sea salt and freshly ground black pepper

½ bulb fennel

2 cups baby arugula

GRAPEFRUIT VINAIGRETTE

¼ cup fresh grapefruit juice

1½ tablespoons white wine vinegar

½ cup extra virgin olive oil

Sea salt and freshly ground black pepper

To make the salad: Preheat a grill to high heat, or prepare a charcoal grill until the coals are bright red.

In a large bowl, combine the lemon zest and juice, olive oil, garlic, red pepper flakes, and parsley. Add the calamari and toss. Let marinate for 30 minutes.

Supreme the grapefruit and squeeze the membranes over a medium bowl. (See note on supreming, page 45.) Reserve the juices for the vinaigrette (see below).

Remove the calamari from the marinade and skewer them. Season the calamari with salt and pepper to taste and grill them about 2 minutes per side, until slightly charred and opaque. (You can also use a hot cast iron skillet on the stove to cook the calamari. Shake the excess marinade from the calamari and sear on each side for 2 minutes.) Using a mandoline, shave the fennel bulb into thin slices. In a large bowl, combine the calamari, fennel, arugula, and grapefruit segments.

To make the grapefruit vinaigrette: To the bowl with the membrane-squeezed grapefruit juice, whisk in the vinegar and olive oil. Season with salt and pepper to taste.

Add the vinaigrette to the large bowl with the calamari and toss. Season to taste and serve immediately.

OCTOPUS SALAD

INSALATA DI POLPO

• SERVES 6 •

G: *This warm-ish salad makes for a great meal. Octopus requires attention at first, because if you overdo it during the initial cooking, it gets too mushy. You're looking for that window when the octopus has bite, yet breaks in your mouth. Many cooks have their tricks regarding this—including adding a wine cork to the pot, since the cork contains an acid that tenderizes protein. But the trick I subscribe to is adding white wine vinegar to the boil and letting the octopus cool in its own bath of cooking water.*

Kosher salt and freshly ground black pepper

1 large octopus or 2 medium-to-small octopi (about 1 pound total)

2 garlic cloves

1 carrot, roughly chopped

1 celery stalk, roughly chopped

½ cup white wine vinegar

2 russet (baking) potatoes, washed

4 tablespoons extra virgin olive oil

1 cup cherry tomatoes, quartered

5 ounces baby arugula

1 tablespoon finely sliced chives

Juice of 1 lemon, for serving

Bring a large pot of salted water to a boil. Add the octopus, garlic, carrot, celery, and vinegar, stir well, and cover. Reduce the heat to medium-low and cook for 30 to 45 minutes, until tender but still a little firm. Remove from the heat and let the octopus cool in the cooking water for about 30 minutes.

In a large pot, combine the potatoes and cold water and bring to a boil. Cook for 10 to 15 minutes, until just tender. Drain, cool, peel, and cut the potatoes into 1-inch cubes.

In a large skillet, heat 2 tablespoons of the oil over medium-high heat until hot. Add the potatoes and season lightly with salt and pepper. Cook for 7 to 10 minutes, until browned on all sides. Add the tomatoes and toss for 1 minute, or until softened. Set aside.

Using a knife, remove the head from the octopus and cut the tentacles into ½-inch pieces. If you use the head, remove the teeth and cartilage with a paring knife. Cut the head into thin strips no more than 1½ inches long.

In a large skillet, heat the remaining 2 tablespoons olive oil over high heat until just smoking. Add the chopped octopus in a single layer, lightly season with salt and pepper, and cook undisturbed for 5 to 6 minutes, until well seared on one side. Flip and cook an additional 5 minutes to sear the other side. Remove from the heat.

On a platter, make a bed of the arugula and top with the potatoes and the octopus. Sprinkle with the chives and dress with the lemon juice.

CUCUMBER, BEET, AND BOTTARGA SALAD

INSALATA DI CETRIOLO, BIETOLE E BOTTARGA

—•| SERVES 2 |•—

D: *The dried, salted fish roe known in Italy as* bottarga *sometimes gets called "the poor man's caviar," but it makes for a great salty, summery salad topping. The other thing to keep in mind about this salad is the importance of washing your knife and your hands after plating each serving of beets. Otherwise, the beet color will bleed into the cucumber and turn your cucumber purple!*

1 medium beet, peeled

Kosher salt and freshly ground
   black pepper

1 English cucumber, halved and seeded

2 tablespoons extra virgin olive oil

Grated zest and juice of 1 lemon

1 handful fresh mint leaves, finely
   chopped, plus whole leaves for garnish

1 tablespoon bottarga

In a medium pot, combine the beet with water to cover. Salt lightly and bring to a boil. Cook for about 20 minutes until tender, then remove from the water and set aside to cool.

Using a mandoline with a julienne blade, first slice the cucumber into very thin strings. Then slice the beet into very thin rings. (The cucumber is first, since the beet will stain the mandoline.)

In a small measuring cup, mix together the olive oil, lemon juice, and mint. Add salt and pepper to taste. Whisk until the mixture is emulsified. It should look opaque, with a bright yellow/green color.

In each of 2 salad bowls, place strings of cucumber and rings of beet. Try to give as much height and dimension as possible—you could even use tweezers.

Shave ½ tablespoon bottarga on top of each cucumber/beet serving. Lightly sprinkle each serving with the dressing. Garnish with lemon zest and whole mint leaves on top, and serve.

meat

CARNE

G: One of the more surprising discoveries I made when I moved to Los Angeles to be with Deborah was how cheap supermarket meat was. I was instantly suspicious. It felt cheap, too. It was already separating from the bone. The texture was off, not what I'd known from my experiences in Tuscany. Then again, Italians do not buy their beef, veal, chicken, or pork in small plastic-wrapped packages with a sticker on it. We go to, love, and rely on butchers, trained purveyors in their locality's best animal products. They know everything about what they're selling, and what you—the loyal customer—are looking for. I have noticed that butchers have become something of a specialty trend for the food-conscious in America. I see these small, boutique *macellerie* (butcher shops) popping up, and the vibe is that this is a pricey alternative for high-end shoppers. But it's not, and it shouldn't be. Butchers are what every community needs if we're going to curb the explosion of mass-produced, hormone- and-antibiotic-ridden, environmentally unsound meat.

The epiphany our family had about cheap meat happened on a road trip we took from Los Angeles to the Bay Area. The fast, direct route is up the I-5, and there's a miles-long stretch where all you see are cows with no pasture. There were thousands of them, crammed together, with what looked like no grass for them to eat. On our return trip, we took the longer, hillier, more scenic route via the Pacific Coast Highway, and we saw real pastures, and cows eating grass with plenty of room. That's when I realized, these are the cows whose cuts are being sold for a higher price at a butcher, and the cows on the I-5 are the ones yielding meat in plastic wrap at the supermarket. I thought, how do I want my food grown? Rolling in filth? Or in green grass? Because in the end, you are what you eat.

So we stopped being stingy about meat with our budget. We eat less of it, and save our dollars for the higher-quality, organic kind a butcher has to offer. Getting to know your local butcher will change your life. And if there's not a butcher in your area, try your farmers' market, which will likely feature purveyors selling locally raised meat and poultry. You'll learn more about different cuts and where the meat comes from. And if you ask, they'll tell you the best ways to cook what they're selling. The more you turn food-purchasing into an active relationship between you and the people you get your food from, the more enjoyable and healthy your eating life will be. So find your butcher and help keep that operation going. It's one of the truest ways you can live like a Tuscan!

BEEF TARTARE

TARTARA DI MANZO

· SERVES 4 ·

G: *If ever a dish needed to stand on the quality of the meat, it's this one. I remember birthday celebrations with my parents at this fancy Florentine restaurant, where the tartare would be prepared tableside like a little show, the waiter mixing the raw beef with egg yolk, capers, and onions, all right in front of us. As I got older though, I preferred to strip away the extra flavors and make it about the meat, complemented by the tartness of lemon. Think of this as a "tequila shot" of tasty beef: salt, pepper, lemon juice, and it's down the hatch!*

4 lemons, 2 cut into ¼-inch-thick slices and 2 zested

1 pound center-cut beef filet

Sea salt and freshly ground black pepper

Preheat a griddle over high heat.

Sear the lemon slices on the griddle for just under 2 minutes per side until they become slightly caramelized. Remove from the heat and set aside.

Using a sharp knife, coarsely mince the filet. Form the meat into 8 loose, walnut-size balls, about 2 ounces each. Place each serving on a seared slice of lemon.

Serve immediately with lemon zest and salt and pepper.

IMPORTANTE! Eye of round makes for a worthy substitution as a beef cut for tartare. Plus, it's a more economy-minded choice than filet.

FLORENTINE STEAK

BISTECCA ALLA FIORENTINA

—— SERVES 2–4 ——

G: *When we talk in my homeland about this glorious T-bone crossroads of strip loin and filet, scents and taste memories instantly come to mind: bone-in steak thick enough to look prehistoric; the orange-white tint of blazing hot charcoal; the mouthwatering aroma of a perfect charring in progress; the ruby red inside that indicates a perfectly rare doneness; and the noble flavor that comes from those luscious bites. As you get ready to embark on this elemental journey of beef, seasoning, and fire, remember that the steak should be at room temperature before cooking, and it's best to season right before grilling so the salt doesn't pull water out of the beef. And for the carnivores in your circle who prefer their cow more pink than tuna-sushi-red, the outer portions of this hefty cut will be more to their liking, while the parts closer to the bone will be rarer. Pass that bone around at the end, too—the hardcore eaters will get a few bites sweet enough to be like meat candy!*

1 porterhouse steak, at least 2 inches thick, kept at room temperature for 1 hour 30 minutes before cooking

1 tablespoon sea salt

1 tablespoon freshly ground black pepper

Preheat a grill to high heat, or prepare a charcoal grill until the coals are bright red.

Right before cooking, season the steak with the salt and pepper on both sides. Place on the grill and cook until well charred, about 6 minutes on one side, then 6 minutes on the other side. You're looking for a nice char on the outside and rare on the inside, which is the traditional Fiorentina style. (If you prefer medium, cook each side for 8 minutes; cook longer per side for well-done.)

Remove the meat from the grill and let it rest for 10 minutes.

Carve the strip steak off one side of the bone, and the filet from the other. Slice the meat against the grain and serve with the bone.

GRILLED TUSCAN CHICKEN

POLLO AL MATTONE

SERVES 6–8

D: *When you flatten a well-marinated chicken on a grill with a brick, you're accomplishing two key things: the brick absorbing heat and giving it back to the chicken, especially if you're grilling outdoors; and letting the direct fire brand your chicken with a wonderful sear, which makes the skin so fantastically crispy that it becomes like a chicken chip!*

2 tablespoons fresh rosemary, chopped

3 lemons, 2 juiced and 1 sliced, for serving

½ cup extra virgin olive oil

Kosher salt and freshly ground black pepper

2 (3½-pound) whole chickens

1 cup arugula

In a large resealable plastic bag, combine the rosemary, lemon juice, olive oil, and salt and pepper to taste.

Using kitchen shears, cut the backbone out of the chicken. (If you make chicken stock, you can save the backbone in the freezer.) Lay out the chickens, skin-side up on a flat surface and firmly press down on them with the heels of your hands to flatten. Add the chickens to the bagged marinade and refrigerate for at least 3 hours or up to overnight.

Preheat a grill to medium-high heat, or prepare a charcoal grill until the coals are bright red.

Remove the chickens from the marinade and place skin-side down on the grill rack.

Place a foil-covered brick on top of each chicken. Grill for 20 minutes, then remove the bricks and flip the chicken. Replace the bricks and grill for 15 to 20 minutes longer, until the chicken is cooked through, with an internal temperature of 165°F. (Check either the center of the breast or the thigh right above the drumstick.) Remove from the grill and let rest for 5 minutes.

Carve the chicken and serve immediately on a bed of the arugula and lemon slices.

SUPER TUSCAN BURGER

G: *When I was fifteen years old, the very first burger joint opened in Florence, and I remember how that became the Saturday afternoon high school hangout. My friends and I would sit down and pretend we were in* Happy Days, *with our milkshakes and burgers.*

D: *As in, Fonzie* Happy Days? *Is that why you were starstruck when I introduced you to my friend Henry Winkler?*

G: *Well . . . yes.*

D: *That is so cute!*

G: *The thing I never understood about American burgers, however, is that there's never any attention to the patty. It's all about the lettuce, the tomato, the sauce. . . .*

D: *You mean ketchup, Gabriele. There's no ketchup in Italy. Your country doesn't like ketchup.*

G: *Too much ketchup makes every burger taste the same. It's all thickness and layers and cheese, but what about the patty? That's the most important part! A great burger has to be about the meat. When I came to America, I wanted to do something special with the patty, so I treated it like a meatloaf, with onion and egg yolk and parsley. That's one of the first ways I figured out how to adapt the kind of food Americans like to my Tuscan heritage.*

D: *And I was a happy guinea pig. You know, I wasn't much of a meat eater until I got pregnant and started craving meat. This burger did the trick.*

1 pound ground beef

¼ red onion, finely chopped

1 tablespoon finely chopped fresh Italian parsley

1 large egg yolk

1 tablespoon freshly grated Pecorino cheese

Kosher salt and freshly ground black pepper

4 slices provolone cheese

4 burger buns, split

1 avocado, sliced

4 lettuce leaves

1 tomato, sliced

Preheat a grill to medium-high heat, or prepare a charcoal grill until the coals are bright red.

In a large bowl, combine the meat, onion, parsley, egg yolk, and Pecorino and stir well until all the ingredients are evenly mixed.

Divide the meat mixture into 4 equal pieces and shape them into patties. Season the patties on both sides with salt and pepper. Grill the patties for 3 to 4 minutes on each side for medium-rare. Place the provolone slices on top of the burgers for the final minute of grilling.

Transfer the meat to a large platter and let rest for 5 minutes. Meanwhile, use the grill to lightly toast the buns.

Serve the burgers dressed with the avocado, lettuce, and tomato.

SAUSAGE AND BEANS

SALSICCIE E FAGIOLI

G: *Tuscans like their pork sausage to be made with pig, salt, pepper, and fennel. In America I've seen lots of different flavored sausages, but it's hard to beat the real thing: a savory ode to the rich flavor of pork. Paired with a garlic-based red sauce and cannellini beans, they're a mouthwatering favorite with family and friends. Tuscany on a plate!*

2 tablespoons extra virgin olive oil

8 pork sausages

5 garlic cloves, cut into chunks

1 teaspoon hot red pepper flakes

1 (28-ounce) can whole peeled tomatoes (pelati)

Salt and freshly ground black pepper

5 fresh bay leaves

2 (15-ounce) cans cannellini beans, drained and rinsed

2 tablespoons chopped fresh Italian parsley

In a large sauté pan, heat the olive oil over medium-high heat until hot. Add the sausages and cook for 8 minutes, or until browned on all sides. Remove from the pan and let the sausages rest on a platter. (As an alternative, the sausages can be broiled in the oven for the same amount of time.)

Add the garlic to the pan and sauté for 1 minute, or until golden brown. Add the red pepper flakes and stir for 1 minute. Break up the tomatoes by hand and add to the pan. Season with salt and black pepper to taste, stir with a wooden spoon, reduce the heat to medium-low, and partially cover the pan with a lid. Simmer for 10 minutes, or until the tomatoes have broken down and thickened to a saucelike consistency.

Add the browned sausages—along with any juices from the plate—and the bay leaves, and cook for 15 to 20 minutes. Add the beans, stir well, and simmer for another 10 minutes to heat through and blend the flavors.

Transfer to plates and garnish with chopped parsley before serving.

ROAST PIG

PORCHETTA

SERVES 10–12

G: *You know what my definition of torture is? Having a secret taste for pork and being in the car with my kosher Jewish father while he drives by a* porchetta *stand, selling hunks of absolutely delicious, rosemary-sage-and-garlic-infused roasted pig, usually in panini. Porchetta sandwiches are to soccer matches in Italy what tailgate party hamburgers and concession hot dogs are to football games in America. Porchetta is a true religion in Italy, but it's also a symbol of liberation to me, two times over—first, when I got my own motorbike and could go straight to the stadium porchetta truck, and second, when I mastered a recipe for it. Pork butt (aka shoulder) will make for a delicious porchetta-style roast, with plenty left over for sandwiches the next day. Just make sure you get it with the fat. You want that flavor! Oven-Roasted Potatoes (page 193) are a perfect accompaniment.*

3 tablespoons roughly chopped fresh sage leaves

2 tablespoons roughly chopped fresh rosemary

2 heads garlic, halved horizontally, plus 5 garlic cloves

½ tablespoon fennel seeds, lightly crushed

3 tablespoons extra virgin olive oil, plus more for brushing and drizzling

1 tablespoon kosher salt, plus more for seasoning

2 teaspoons freshly ground black pepper, plus more for seasoning

1 (6½-pound) boneless pork butt (pork shoulder)

2 baby potatoes, halved

1 cup dry white wine

Preheat the oven to 325°F.

In a food processor, combine the sage, rosemary, the 5 garlic cloves, fennel seeds, olive oil, and salt and pepper and blend until a paste forms. (You can also mash these ingredients together with a mortar and pestle.)

Using a sharp knife, butterfly the pork butt, so it opens up like a book. (You can also have your butcher do this for you.) Rub the inside cut of the meat with the paste. Using kitchen twine, tie the butterflied pork back together to make a compact shape (see page 150).

Place the halved garlic heads and potatoes, cut-sides down, on the bottom of a roasting pan to create a bed for the pork butt so it doesn't sit directly on the surface of the pan. Place the pork fat-side up on the bed of garlic and potatoes, drizzle lightly with olive oil, and season with salt and pepper to taste.

(continued)

Place the pan in the oven and bake for 5 hours, or until the skin is browned and the meat is extremely tender; pour the wine over the pork after the first 30 minutes of roasting and baste the meat with the collected pan juices every 40 minutes.

Remove from the oven and let rest for 20 minutes. Remove the twine before cutting the pork into ½-inch-thick slices.

IMPORTANTE! After slow-roasting the pork, the garlic should be soft. Spread it on bread for an appetizer. The potatoes make for a nice cook's treat—snack on them while you're waiting for the pork to rest.

FLORENTINE OSSO BUCO

OSSO BUCO ALLA FIORENTINA

SERVES 4

D: *This tender, slow-cooking classic from Milan typically gets paired with a risotto, but in Tuscany we like it with roasted potatoes or sautéed greens. We also use red wine instead of white, because of our beloved Sangiovese grapes. The gremolata is a chopped herb mixture for the dish, and it should really be fresh, so make it in the hour before the osso buco is ready, never earlier in the day or the night before.*

OSSO BUCO

4 (¾-pound) ossi buchi (beef or veal shanks)

1 tablespoon unsalted butter

2 tablespoons extra virgin olive oil

1 small white or yellow onion, finely chopped

2 cups beef broth

Flour, for dusting

½ cup dry red wine

Kosher salt and freshly ground black pepper

GREMOLATA

1 garlic clove, finely chopped

1 handful fresh Italian parsley, finely chopped

Grated zest of 1 lemon

To make the osso buco: Using a paring knife, make a few small incisions around the ossi buchi. (This prevents the meat from curling up during cooking.)

In a large skillet, heat the butter and olive oil over medium-high heat until the butter is melted. Add the onion and cook for 2 to 3 minutes, or until softened.

Meanwhile, in a small pot, bring the broth to a boil, then set it aside to be used when warm.

Dust the ossi buchi with flour. Place them in the skillet and cook for 5 to 6 minutes on each side. Add the wine and cook until reduced to less than half, about 5 minutes. Add the broth and reduce the heat to medium-low. Season the meat with salt and pepper to taste. Partially cover and cook for 1 hour 30 minutes, shaking the pan occasionally to prevent the meat from sticking to the bottom, until the meat is fall-off-the-bone tender.

Meanwhile, **to make the gremolata:** In a small bowl, combine the garlic, parsley, and lemon zest.

Stir the gremolata into the osso buco and cook for 3 to 5 minutes. Serve.

ROASTED PORK LOIN

ARISTA ALLA FOCETTINA

SERVES 4–6

G: *My name for this is a dedication of sorts to my L.A. bicycling buddy Marzia, a transplant like me who hails from Focette, a coastal Tuscan town. She helped inspire this dish. The pork gets a wonderful golden color, but it's really all about the sauce. This dish goes wonderfully with Oven-Roasted Potatoes (page 193) and Sautéed Zucchini (page 183).*

¼ cup extra virgin olive oil

5 garlic cloves, unpeeled

3 sprigs fresh rosemary

12 fresh sage leaves

2½ pounds pork loin

1 cup dry white wine

Kosher salt and freshly ground black pepper

½ cup whole milk

In a large Dutch oven, heat the olive oil over medium-high heat until hot. Add the garlic, rosemary, and sage and sauté for 4 to 5 minutes, until the herbs start to crisp.

Add the pork loin, laying it on top of the herbs, and cook for 5 minutes. Turn it over and cook the other side for 5 minutes. Add the wine to the Dutch oven, using a wooden spoon to scrape any browned bits from the bottom. Cook for 1 to 2 minutes, until the scent of alcohol has disappeared.

Reduce the heat to medium-low, season with salt and pepper to taste, and partially cover with the lid. Cook for about 1 hour, turning the meat and scraping the bottom of the pot every 15 to 20 minutes. If the sauce reduces too much, add warm water in small increments, ¼ cup at a time. Remove the pot from the heat and place the pork loin on a cutting board to rest for 30 minutes.

When the sauce in the Dutch oven has cooled, add the milk and cook, stirring constantly to prevent curds from forming, over medium-low heat for 2 to 3 minutes, until the sauce is lightly creamy, but not thick.

Thinly slice the pork loin and serve with the sauce poured on top.

PORK CHOP
with tuscan kale

BISTECCHINA DI MAIALE COL CAVOLO NERO

SERVES 4

D: *Wintertime in Tuscany means celebrating the arrival of* cavolo nero, *which is also known as Tuscan kale or lacinato kale. There is much love for this bitter, earthy leaf in Italy, and it ends up in soups like Ribollita (page 110), or gracing entrees like this one, where it goes wonderfully with the wine-glazed pork chops.*

Kosher salt

2 bunches Tuscan kale (aka lacinato, black kale, cavolo nero), stems removed, roughly chopped

5 tablespoons extra virgin olive oil

3 ounces guanciale, thinly sliced

3 garlic cloves, roughly chopped

Pinch of hot red pepper flakes

1 cup all-purpose flour, for dredging

1 teaspoon freshly ground black pepper

4 (8-ounce) bone-in pork chops

12 fresh sage leaves

¼ cup dry white wine

Bring a 6-quart pot of salted water to a boil. Cook the kale in the boiling water for 4 to 5 minutes, until it wilts but still has a sturdiness. Drain and rinse the kale under cold running water. Squeeze it dry and set aside.

In a large skillet, heat 2 tablespoons of the olive oil over medium-high heat until hot. Add the guanciale and cook for 4 to 5 minutes, until it begins to crisp. Add the garlic and continue to cook for 1 minute, or until the garlic starts to turn golden. Add the red pepper flakes and sauté for 1 minute. Add the kale and toss for 2 minutes. Remove the kale from the heat and set aside.

In a shallow bowl, combine the flour, 1 teaspoon salt, and the black pepper. Dredge the pork chops in the flour mixture.

In a second large skillet, heat the remaining 3 tablespoons olive oil over medium-high heat until hot. Add the pork and sage leaves, cooking 1 side of the chops for 4 minutes, then turning and cooking the other side for 4 minutes. Remove the chops to a plate.

Add the wine to the hot pork chop pan and scrape the bottom with a wooden spoon to release the browned, cooked bits. Cook for 2 minutes, then add the pork chops back to the pan and cook for an additional 5 minutes, until the sauce has reduced by half and the scent of alcohol has disappeared. The pork chops should look crisp on the outside, but still feel soft to the touch.

Serve each chop with some kale, drizzling the chops with the juices from the pan.

BEEF STEW
with polenta

SPEZZATINO DI MANZO

G: *My mother made this comforting stew in a cast iron pot over a fireplace during our Christmas vacations. The flavor base, or soffritto, of onion, carrots, and celery gives your beef the perfect start for slow-cooking. It's a winter warmer, so don't try it in August! The patience it requires is well returned: the meat will just fall apart.*

BEEF STEW

3 tablespoons extra virgin olive oil

1 red onion, diced

3 carrots, cut into ½-inch pieces

3 celery stalks, cut into ½-inch pieces

2 pounds stew beef, such as boneless chuck, trimmed of excess fat and cut into 1½-inch cubes

2½ cups dry red wine

8 sprigs fresh thyme

3 medium tomatoes, halved

Salt and freshly ground black pepper

POLENTA

1 tablespoon extra virgin olive oil

4 cups vegetable stock, homemade (page 94) or store-bought

1 cup instant polenta

To make the stew: In a large, heavy saucepan, heat the olive oil over medium-high heat until hot but not smoking. Add the onion, carrots, and celery and sauté for 10 minutes, until the soffritto is soft and translucent. Add the beef and sauté, stirring occasionally, for 5 minutes, until browned on all sides. Add the wine and thyme, stir well, and bring to a boil.

Add the tomatoes, season with salt and pepper, reduce the heat to medium-low, and simmer partially covered for 2 hours, stirring every 15 minutes, until the beef is tender.

To make the polenta: Coat the inside of a large serving bowl with the olive oil and set aside.

In a large pot, bring the stock to a boil over medium-high heat. Reduce the heat to medium and slowly add the polenta, stirring constantly. Cook for 5 minutes—or however long the box indicates—stirring constantly, until the polenta thickens and pulls away from the sides of the pot. Transfer to the oil-coated bowl and let set for 5 to 10 minutes.

Turn the polenta out of the bowl, slice, and serve alongside the beef stew.

HUNTER'S CHICKEN

POLLO ALLA CACCIATORA

⸺ SERVES 6 ⸺

G: *In my homeland, all the farmers become hunters on Sunday. I remember this hunter's shack on our property that was used to wait for animals. One guy named Mario had a little gas burner and some pots, and during winter he'd bring with him a metal tin—the kind soldiers once used to keep food—containing chicken that his wife had marinated the night before. He would get a* soffritto *going with anchovy and garlic, braise the chicken in the pot, cover it with the marinating sauce and some tomatoes, and cook it all morning while he waited for his unlucky prey. Then, as the sun went down, he'd walk home, rifle in one hand and a meal in the other. That's why* cacciatora *is a hunter's classic, and this is the recipe Mario taught me when I was eight years old.*

3 tablespoons olive oil

12 chicken pieces (a mix of white meat and dark pieces)

Kosher salt and freshly ground black pepper

3 oil-packed anchovy fillets

3 garlic cloves, quartered

2 small red onions, finely chopped

2 carrots, finely chopped

1 celery stalk, finely chopped

1 cup Sangiovese red wine

2½ cups chopped Roma or plum tomatoes

½ cup black olives, pitted

4 fresh bay leaves

3 tablespoons chopped fresh Italian parsley

In a large skillet, heat the olive oil over medium-high heat until hot. Season the chicken with salt and pepper to taste. Add the chicken to the skillet and sear for 4 minutes per side, until golden brown. Transfer to a plate.

Add the anchovies and garlic to the hot skillet, using a wooden spoon to break up the anchovies. Sauté for 2 to 3 minutes, until the garlic is fragrant and the anchovies are melted. Add the onions, carrots, and celery and sauté for 5 to 7 minutes, until tender and just beginning to turn golden. Stir in the wine and cook for 2 minutes, until the scent of alcohol disappears. Add the tomatoes, olives, and bay leaves and stir well to mix the ingredients.

Return the chicken to the skillet and cover with the tomatoes, flipping the pieces to coat them with the sauce. Partially cover, reduce the heat to low, and simmer for 45 to 50 minutes, until the meat looks ready to detach from the bones.

Discard the bay leaves and serve with a sprinkling of the parsley.

FRITTATA ROAST ROLL

ROTOLO CON LA FRITTATA

SERVES 4–6

D: *This is one of your grandmother's specialties, right, Gabriele?*

G: *I can see myself now, being happily sent on my bicycle to her house to pick it up. Other times, we'd see her walking up the path and I couldn't help it, I'd have to go run out and meet her.*

D: *I know why. It's not only delicious, but beautiful. When you slice it after it's done, you get this beautiful spiral of color: wine-darkened beef, yellow frittata, and green of the spinach.*

G: *It's not a complicated recipe, but it requires time to do everything: pounding the beef, making the frittatas, rolling, stringing, and cooking. But the end result is well worth the effort!*

3 large beef cutlets (flank steak)

Kosher salt

1 bunch spinach

6 large eggs

2 tablespoons whole milk

2 tablespoons freshly grated Parmigiano-
 Reggiano cheese

¼ teaspoon freshly ground black pepper

3 tablespoons unsalted butter

2 tablespoons extra virgin olive oil

3 garlic cloves, roughly chopped

1 sprig fresh rosemary

½ cup red wine

Place the beef cutlets between 2 sheets of plastic wrap, or in a plastic bag, and pound them for 30 seconds, making sure not to punch holes in the cutlets.

Bring a pot of salted water to a boil. Add the spinach to the boiling water and cook for 1 minute. Drain and rinse the spinach under cold water, then squeeze it dry, finely chop, and set aside.

In a large bowl, combine the eggs, milk, Parmesan, ½ teaspoon salt, and the pepper. Whisk until evenly mixed. Add the cooked spinach and whisk.

In an 8-inch nonstick skillet, heat 1 tablespoon of the butter until melted. Pour in one-third of the egg batter, cover the pan, and cook over medium-low heat for 5 to 7 minutes, or until the edges of the frittata brown slightly and the top is firm and not runny. Transfer the frittata to a plate to cool. Repeat this step until you have 3 small frittatas.

Place a beef cutlet on a cutting board and top with a frittata. Roll the 2 together and

secure with twine, making sure not to tighten too much, otherwise the twine will break through the beef, or push the frittata out of the roll. Repeat with the remaining beef and frittatas.

In a large skillet, heat the olive oil, garlic, and rosemary over medium-high heat and cook for 2 to 3 minutes, until the rosemary crisps and the garlic starts browning. Add the rolls, searing the meat evenly all over by rolling them in the pan for 4 to 5 minutes.

Add the wine and cook for 3 to 4 minutes, until the scent of alcohol disappears. Reduce the heat to medium-low and cook, partially covered, for 25 to 30 minutes, until the meat looks lightly caramelized on the outside, the rolls are firm, and no juices leak from the rolls when a finger is pressed into them.

Transfer the rolls to a cutting board to rest for up to 5 minutes. Thinly slice and serve with a drizzle of the pan juices.

fish

PESCE

G: Italy is in the middle of the Mediterranean, which makes it a fish lover's paradise. Each region and coastal area has its own celebrated seafood. There's the mainland, the big islands like Sicily and Sardinia, and all the little island paradises that I loved exploring when I was young. Some ports are so tiny that we could approach a fisherman's small boat and buy fish directly from him before he hit shore!

Fishing was the earliest way I connected to food on a deeper level. I experienced a personal joy in catching something and eating it. Starting with the rubber raft we had when I was six years old, and with the boats my father bought that got bigger and bigger as I got older, summers on the water were an integral part of my life. He taught me everything: how to spear, snorkel, lurk, be patient, kill, scale, gut, and rinse. My mom was the grill cook on the boat or on the beach.

We caught branzino, grouper, bass, and red snapper, but fishing for sole was my favorite. I'd float facedown in crystal clear water, waiting for the flickering of dust that indicates the sand-colored sole is moving slowly along the bottom. I'd spear it when I was sure it wasn't looking— the sole has both eyes on the same side, so it might be looking straight up at you. It tasted extra delicious to me because I'd caught it.

Being a part of that cycle of life is what makes seafood such a special dish to me. Tuscans show great respect for the sea's bounty, which is what Deborah and I want to convey with these recipes, whether the fish is being pan-cooked, grilled, fried, simmered in a stew, or served raw. Throughout Italy there is such pride in preparing as simply as possible the gifts of one's local region, and that goes as much for what the fishermen bring to market as what the hunter has bagged or the farmer has harvested.

FISH TACOS

TACOS DI PESCE

(pictured on page 160)

―――――――――――――――――――――― SERVES 6–8 ――――――――――――――――――――――

D: *When it comes to family favorites in our household, this one's right up there.*

G: *After living in Los Angeles for a decade, where tacos are so ingrained in the culture, we wanted to come up with a dish that celebrates our time there, and my deepening connection to the country that adopted me.*

D: *It's a truly interactive dinner when you get kids involved. They get their corn tortilla with a piece of fish, and they can add whatever they want. We like ours with avocado, lettuce, a splash of lemon, and our homemade Pico de Gallo (opposite). Then we combine a little Mediterranean with our Mexican entree by adding white anchovies to radishes for a tasty extra topping.*

G: *Italians often use sparkling water in the batter when frying fish, because the carbonation yields a lighter texture. But I've found that beer makes for a fluffier batter, and a crispier fry.*

1 cup all-purpose flour

½ cup medium-grind semolina flour

½ teaspoon sea salt

¼ teaspoon freshly ground black pepper

1 (12-ounce) bottle lager beer

1 quart canola oil, for frying

2 pounds tilapia, cod, or sole, cut into 12 ½-inch-thick, finger-size strips

12 medium-sized corn tortillas

2 cups shredded iceberg lettuce, for serving

1 avocado, sliced, for serving

Lemon wedges, for serving

Pico de Gallo (recipe follows)

Radishes with White Anchovies (recipe follows)

In a large bowl, whisk together the all-purpose flour, semolina flour, sea salt, and black pepper. Slowly whisk in the beer and set the batter aside.

Preheat the oven to 350°F.

In a deep 14-inch nonstick skillet, add enough oil to come one-third of the way up the sides of the pan. Heat over high heat until a deep-fry thermometer reads 350°F. (You can also test by adding a small piece of bread to the oil. If it browns, the oil is ready.)

Using tongs, dip the fish into the beer batter, allowing the excess to drip off, and carefully slide into the hot oil. Fry 6 pieces at a time for 6 to 10 minutes, turning the pieces as they cook, until they are golden brown and fish is cooked through. Using a spider or slotted spoon, remove the pieces from the oil, and place on a paper towel–lined baking sheet to drain.

Meanwhile, wrap the tortillas in foil and heat in the oven for 10 minutes.

To serve, place a fried fish strip on a warmed tortilla. Top with shredded lettuce and an avocado slice. Serve with lemon wedges, pico de gallo, and the radishes with anchovies.

IMPORTANTE! If you see the bottom of the pan turning dark with batter residue, start over with fresh oil. (This tends to happen after 2 pounds of fish have been fried.)

PICO DE GALLO
MAKES 3 CUPS

1½ pounds mixed heirloom tomatoes, not overly ripe, medium diced

½ small red onion, finely diced (about ½ cup)

½ bunch cilantro, stems removed, roughly chopped

3 tablespoons capers, rinsed and chopped

3 tablespoons extra virgin olive oil

Juice of 1 lemon

Sea salt and freshly ground black pepper

In a large bowl, combine the tomatoes, onion, cilantro, capers, olive oil, and lemon juice. Toss well and season with salt and pepper to taste.

RADISHES WITH WHITE ANCHOVIES
RAPINI E ACCIUGHE
SERVES 6–8

1 bunch radishes, well scrubbed, tops trimmed, halved or quartered lengthwise, cut into half or quarter moons

½ pound marinated white anchovy fillets, cut into strips

¼ cup fresh Italian parsley leaves, chopped

2 tablespoons extra virgin olive oil

Salt and freshly ground black pepper

In a medium bowl, combine the radishes, anchovies, parsley, and olive oil, and toss well. Season with salt and pepper to taste.

TUNA TARTARE

TARTARE DI TONNO

· SERVES 6–8 ·

D: *I love the clean, fresh taste of sushi-grade tuna, and when it's diced and decorated with mint, basil, and lemon, it's the perfect* aperitivo *with a glass of white wine or Prosecco. If you're planning a big party, it's worth noting that you can dice the tuna in advance, keep it refrigerated, and dress it right before serving.*

2 tuna steaks (¾ pound each), 1¼ inches thick, finely diced

2 lemons, 1 zested and 1 cut into wedges for squeezing

10 fresh mint leaves, finely sliced (chiffonade-style), plus sprigs for garnish

6 fresh basil leaves, finely sliced (chiffonade-style), plus sprigs for garnish

Sea salt and freshly ground black pepper

2 tablespoons extra virgin olive oil (optional)

Flatbread crackers, broken into bite-size pieces

In a large bowl, combine the tuna, lemon zest, mint, and basil, and stir gently. Season with salt and pepper to taste. If using olive oil, add it now.

Spoon generous portions of the tartare onto the cracker pieces.

Serve immediately with a squeeze of lemon, and garnish with the mint and basil sprigs.

DRUNKEN TUNA

TONNO UBRIACO

We call this tuna "drunken" because of the red wine. But we could also call the dish a tuna cacciatore—it treats this meaty fish as if it were as worthy of a hearty inland stew as meat or fowl. It has a burst of color with the red wine, tomatoes, and the bright red tuna. Serve this with a crunchy side like Oven-Roasted Potatoes (page 193), or a crisp kale salad.

4 (½-pound) tuna steaks, rinsed

1 cup all-purpose flour, for dusting

¼ cup extra virgin olive oil, plus more if needed

1 red onion, ¾ finely chopped, ¼ thinly sliced

2 garlic cloves, roughly chopped

⅔ cup canned whole peeled tomatoes (pelati), puréed in a blender

2 ounces black olives, pitted, sliced medium-thin

½ cup red wine

Salt and freshly ground black pepper

1 handful fresh Italian parsley, finely chopped

Lightly dust the tuna steaks with the flour.

In a deep 14-inch nonstick skillet, heat the olive oil over medium-high heat until hot. Add the tuna steaks and sear for 2 minutes per side, until browned. Then remove the tuna steaks from the pan and set aside on a plate lined with parchment paper.

Add the chopped and sliced onion to the same skillet and sauté for 3 to 4 minutes, until soft and golden. Add the garlic and cook for 2 minutes, until it's fragrant and softened. Add the tomatoes, olives, and wine. Reduce the heat to medium and cook for 10 minutes, until the sauce starts to thicken. Return the tuna to the pan, season with salt and pepper to taste, reduce the heat to medium-low, and cook for 3 to 4 minutes to heat the tuna through.

Transfer the tuna to plates and top with the sauce. Garnish with the parsley and serve.

SWORDFISH ROLLS

INVOLTINI DI PESCE SPADA

· SERVES 6 ·

G: *My grandfather introduced me to the seaside restaurant that brought swordfish out on yellow paper, golden-edged and crispy on the outside, rich and meaty on the inside. This recipe is my southern Italian–influenced take on the fish, something to make for a big family get-together, or for a celebratory event, since it requires some effort. If you're surprised to see grated cheese in a fish dish, you'll be just as surprised to discover that the Pecorino, bread crumbs, and capers work beautifully as a filling. These rolls are a mouthful that scream for beer, so have some chilled brews handy!*

6 tablespoons extra virgin olive oil

1 shallot, chopped medium-fine

2 garlic cloves, roughly chopped

½ teaspoon hot red pepper flakes

½ pound swordfish scraps (ask your fishmonger for these)

½ cup white wine

1 handful fresh Italian parsley, roughly chopped, plus more for garnish

Salt and freshly ground black pepper

⅓ cup freshly grated aged Pecorino cheese

1 tablespoon capers, rinsed

½ cup dried bread crumbs, plus more for sprinkling

1½ pounds swordfish, cut into 12 (¼-inch-thick) steaks (have your fishmonger do this)

1 lemon, cut into 6 wedges, for serving

In a deep 14-inch skillet, heat 2 tablespoons of the oil over medium-high heat until hot. Add the shallot and sauté for 4 minutes, until softened. Add the garlic and sauté for 1 minute.

Add the red pepper flakes and stir, then add the swordfish scraps. Using a wooden spoon, break them down in the skillet. Add the wine and parsley, season with salt and pepper to taste, and cook for 3 to 5 minutes, until the sauce has reduced by one-third. Remove the swordfish scraps from the heat and reserve.

In a 2-quart bowl, combine the Pecorino, capers, bread crumbs, and cooked swordfish scraps. Season lightly with salt and pepper and add 2 tablespoons of the olive oil.

Preheat the oven to 350°F.

Place 1 tablespoon of the bread crumb mixture in the center of each swordfish slice, then wrap the fish around it and secure with a toothpick. Place the rolls in a 9 × 13-inch baking dish and sprinkle with the remaining 2 tablespoons olive oil, and salt and pepper to taste. Sprinkle with more bread crumbs and place in the oven. Bake for about 15 minutes, until crisp on the outside and the flesh is golden.

Serve with lemon wedges and a sprinkle of parsley.

LIVORNO-STYLE MIXED FISH STEW

CACIUCCO ALLA LIVORNESE

· SERVES 8–10 ·

D: *This caciucco is a traditional fish stew from Livorno that highlights scraps that were unsold by the fishmonger at the end of the day. He took his "small catch" home to a fresh red sauce made by his wife. Of course, in Italy, Gabriele might use cuttlefish, John Dory, scorpion fish, and dogfish, which aren't readily available through your local fishmonger or market. Alternatives are suggested in the ingredients list below. Sliced, toasted Pane Toscano (page 216) makes a great accompaniment to your caciucco.*

3 tablespoons extra virgin olive oil

1 red onion, roughly chopped

5 garlic cloves, chopped medium-fine

5 fresh sage leaves

2 handfuls fresh Italian parsley, roughly chopped

1 teaspoon hot red pepper flakes

½ cup red wine

1 pound octopus, cleaned, beak removed

2 cups canned whole peeled tomatoes (pelati), puréed in a blender

Salt and freshly ground black pepper

2½ pounds local fisherman's small catch (possibly red mullet, crawfish, whiting, hake, squid, eel), cleaned, descaled if necessary, rinsed, cut into 1½-inch chunks

½ pound prawns (or mantis shrimp, if you can find them), preferably with the shells on

In a 16-quart pot, heat the olive oil over medium-high heat until hot. Add the onion and sauté for 5 minutes, or until softened but not darkened. Add the garlic, sage, half the parsley, and the red pepper flakes and stir for 1 minute, until the sage crisps a bit but before the red pepper starts burning. Add the wine and cook for 3 to 4 minutes, until the scent of alcohol disappears.

Add the octopus and stir for 3 to 4 minutes. Add the puréed tomatoes, season with salt and pepper to taste, and stir. Bring it to a soft boil, reduce the heat to medium-low, and cook for 30 minutes, until the octopus is tender. Remove the octopus, cut the tentacles into chunks, slice the head into ½-inch strips, and return the octopus pieces to the pot. Add the fisherman's small catch fish and cook for another 15 to 20 minutes until they're cooked through. Add the prawns and cook another 10 minutes until pink. Add hot water as needed, a ladleful at a time, to keep the fish covered and the soup from thickening too much.

Transfer to soup bowls, garnish with the remaining parsley, and serve.

COD FLORENTINE-STYLE

BACCALÀ ALLA FIORENTINA

D: *This affordable, fragrant dish—a favorite with our kids—is one of those coastal Tuscan specialties that travelled inland from Livorno to Florence. By lightly cooking salt cod in rosemary and garlic, then reinvigorating the* soffritto *with onions, leeks, and tomatoes, the flavors meld in a wonderful way. It's a great hot-weather meal, and pairs nicely with Sautéed Dandelion Greens with Garlic (page 182) or Oven-Roasted Potatoes (page 193). Advance planning is important though, because salt cod needs to soak in cold water at least overnight before cooking.*

2 pounds skin-on salt cod, covered in cold water, refrigerated overnight, rinsed, and deboned

2 cups all-purpose flour, for dredging

5 tablespoons extra virgin olive oil, plus more for serving

4 garlic cloves, roughly chopped

1 sprig fresh rosemary

½ red onion, finely chopped

1 small leek, white part only, well rinsed and finely chopped

1 (28-ounce) can whole peeled tomatoes (pelati)

Salt and freshly ground black pepper

2 tablespoons roughly chopped fresh Italian parsley

Cut the salt cod into roughly 2 × 3-inch pieces.

Spread the flour in a shallow bowl. Dredge the cod pieces and set aside.

In a large nonstick skillet, heat 2 tablespoons of the olive oil over medium-high heat until hot. Add 1 of the chopped garlic cloves and the rosemary sprig and sauté for 2 minutes, until the garlic is fragrant but not dark. Add the floured cod pieces and fry lightly on both sides, about 4 minutes per side, until golden and crisp. Remove the fish and drain on a platter lined with paper towels.

In the same pan, heat the remaining 3 tablespoons olive oil until hot. Add the onion and leek and sauté for 7 to 10 minutes, until softened and lightly browned. Add the remaining garlic, and cook for an additional 2 minutes, until the garlic is fragrant but not dark.

Using your hands, break apart the tomatoes and add them to the soffritto. Season with salt and pepper, reduce the heat to medium-low, and cook for 25 minutes, stirring occasionally, until the sauce has reduced by one-third.

Add the fried salt cod, being careful not to break apart the pieces, and cook for 5 minutes to heat through. Remove the pan from the heat and set aside for 5 minutes.

Serve warm with a garnish of parsley, a drizzle of olive oil, and seasoned with pepper to taste.

SEARED GROUPER OVER FREGOLA
with fava beans and heirloom tomatoes

CERNIA CON FREGOLA E FAVA

— SERVES 4 —

G: *Grouper has always been incredibly hard to catch by hand, because it lives in deep rock cliff caves. The upside is grouper is incredibly light and fluffy. I pair it with fresh heirloom tomatoes and fava beans, then add fregola, also known as Sardinian pasta. This is a vessel-heavy cooking process, so if it helps, make the grains in advance, then reheat them by sautéing with the fava beans during the step involving the tomato.*

1 cup shucked fava beans (from ½ pound fava pods)

3 cups fish stock or shellfish stock (ask your local fishmonger)

Pinch of saffron threads

1 cup fregola or Israeli couscous

3 tablespoons extra virgin olive oil

4 (4- to 6-ounce) skin-on grouper fillets, pin bones removed

Salt and freshly ground black pepper

1 small leek (white and light green parts only), well rinsed, halved lengthwise, and cut crosswise into ⅓-inch-thick half-moons

1 red heirloom tomato, diced small

Bring a medium pot of water to a boil. Add the beans and blanch for 3 minutes. Drain and rinse under cold water. When cool, peel the skin from the beans and set aside.

In a 4-quart saucepan, bring the fish stock and 2 cups water to a boil. Reduce to a simmer and add the saffron and fregola. Cook the fregola until al dente, according to the package directions. Drain, reserving the broth. Set aside the fregola.

In a 14-inch nonstick skillet, heat 2 tablespoons of the oil over medium-high heat until hot. Season both sides of the fillets generously with salt and pepper. Sear the fish, skin-side down, for 6 to 8 minutes, until the skin is crispy and the fish is cooked two-thirds of the way. Flip and cook the other side for about 3 minutes, until cooked through.

Return the saffron broth to a simmer.

In a small skillet, heat the remaining 1 tablespoon olive oil until hot. Add the leek and sauté for 2 minutes, or until soft. Add the reserved fava beans, the tomato, and a pinch of salt. Stir well, cook for 2 minutes, and remove from the heat.

Transfer the fregola to shallow soup bowls and top with the fava bean mixture. Place the seared fish on top and drizzle with a spoonful of the saffron broth.

IMPORTANTE! Wild striped bass makes a good alternative to grouper in this recipe.

I BOSCONI—OUR HOUSE IN TUSCANY

G: Fiesole. There are few words that accurately describe the feeling we get from being on the two hundred acres where I grew up. The right word would somehow incorporate the effect of light on our hills, the rich tradition rising from our land, and the warmth we feel as a family when surrounded by it all. (Is that word "Tuscan" perhaps?)

"I Bosconi" is the name of the estate my great-grandfather Chimici bought in the early part of the twentieth century, and that is now owned by my grandmother. Fiesole is in the heart of Tuscany—it's an ancient Etruscan town nestled in the hills north of Florence, directly opposite the legendary Chianti Mountains. Our hills aren't as sensual and soft as the rolling kind that surround Siena to the south—they're pointier, a little rougher and steeper, but no less beautiful in their natural sweep and majesty. It was blanketed by saffron flowers thousands of years ago when the Etruscans ruled, and as time passed and smaller farms sprouted across it, it transformed into a vast olive orchard and vineyard. When I think about that, it's easy

to imagine how our little region could be so eternally enchanting.

I grew up in one of the property's many farmhouses, built in the 1200s. But where Deborah and I stay now is across the field from my childhood home, in what was once the main estate, first built by the rich family who purchased the land in 1669. It's a huge, square, opulent construction—divided into residential space, livestock rooms, and a place for olives to be unloaded before they are sent to be pressed. When the land changed hands to my great-grandfather, it was still a fully operational collection of farms. He restored the church on the property and invited the priest from Fiesole to celebrate mass there on Saturday afternoons for the farmers who didn't have the means to get into town on Sunday mornings. The idea was to create a sense of community, and some of my

earliest memories are of that bond, watching Nonna Lola and the farmers' wives making pies, jams, preserves, and sauces with the bounty from the land.

My parents still live in the large farmhouse I grew up in. They spent thirty years restoring it, and like a lot of houses on the land, it's well shaded by the beautiful cypresses, pines, and oaks that people have planted over the years. My father and I used to walk the property in winter with a barrel and a couple of shovels and look for tiny tree seedlings. We'd cut the baby tree, take care of it, and eventually plant it on the side of our house. I'd do the same with flowers. It was a mission of mine every April to collect irises, extract the bulbs, tend to them in the garage, then plant them in winter all around the house. Now, every spring, whenever my parents encounter a rich, full bloom of flowers around the olive trees in their garden, they think of me, and the thousands of miles between us don't seem as far.

Feelings like those inspire me to bring our land back to its full potential. The 18,000 olive trees still produce tons of fruit, and are the source of the extra virgin olive oil we sell locally to pay for the farm operations. It's only a matter of time before we realize our dream of not only selling our olive oil on the American market, but getting the vineyard running again—we lost all the grapevines to a snowstorm in 1985. I dream a lot when I'm back in Fiesole: walking with my family along the same paths I ran up and down as a kid, making the meals that reconnect me to the land, enjoying the scents and sights I remember. But that's what the earth is good at— replenishing itself, and giving those who tend it well a chance to make dreams come true.

D: I had never been to Fiesole when I met Gabriele, but like so many tucked-away villages and towns in the heartland of Italy, it felt utterly magical when I first encountered it. Ten minutes by car and up the hill from the pulsing heartbeat of big-city Florence, and I was caught up in the seemingly endless expanse of farmland, magnificent views, and olive trees that reflect silver in the light.

On our property, the scent of cypress hangs in the air and awakens the senses. Manicured gardens inspire long, delightfully meandering walks. Fruit trees invite one to pick and enjoy. Someone will pop open a bottle of Prosecco, and a table is set up outside. Gabriele's Nonna Lola drops by with a welcoming plate of her special biscotti. On an early trip there, I got up the nerve to knock on her door, hoping to spend some quality alone time with her. She barely spoke

any English, and my Italian was earnest but lacking. She showed me her place, let me watch her cook, and then we sat on her patio and had cocktails. Despite the language barrier, we could both sense a common bond that went beyond words, and if I do say so myself, we became fast girlfriends that day.

I've always felt a spiritual kinship with deeply historical places, so it didn't surprise me that I could feel the energy of the Etruscans and their colonizers, the Romans, when I set foot in my husband's hometown. Those early peoples had a link to the earth they tilled that was palpable as I walked the fields. But roaming "I Bosconi" also put me in touch with somebody I once was, a ten-year-old living on her hippie mother's Catskills farm, exploring the woods, crossing fields and streams, and drinking in wildlife. As I got older, I couldn't wait to embrace the big city, but when I settled in as an adult, I remember thinking, "Why was I in such a rush to get away from gorgeous nature?" My husband's childhood home reconnected me to that feeling in an important, soulful way.

On our estate in Tuscany, there's a rich melding of the sculpted and the wild, an architecturally dazzling villa from which a short stroll introduces you to plenty of fresh herbs, fruits, and vegetables. (Maybe even the occasional pheasant, hare, deer, or wild boar!) It's enough to make you think, this is how we were all meant to live, nestled in Mother Nature's embrace, wedded to the very spot our food comes from. The arugula that punches up today's salad. The rosemary that enhances whatever's roasting on the fire. The berry vines and fruit trees that will yield the flavor to follow dinner.

Who's ready for a trip?

vegetables

VERDURE

D: Growing up, vegetables were common at our dinner table but not exactly celebrated for what they were beyond being a necessary source of nutrients. I knew they were good for us, but they weren't always flavorful. Steaming was the only cooking method I remember. What Gabriele and his Tuscan upbringing showed me was how the real, true taste of a country vegetable was in itself a wonderful thing, a bite worthy of enjoying as much as anything else on the plate. Italians don't just steam vegetables: They sauté, bake, and grill them. They make delicious antipasti bites, use them to give heft to soups and salads, to enhance the warming auras of pasta and risotto dishes,

and to provide delicious accompaniment to countless meat, poultry, and fish entrees. They also stand on their own quite nicely.

G: I married a woman who couldn't imagine life without vegetables, but as a kid, I didn't care for them. As I got older and wiser—waking up to the deliciousness that was literally growing in my own backyard!—I came to an understanding about kids and vegetables. Let kids meet you halfway. My daughters hated artichokes, so I stopped serving them, and gave them vegetables they did like. Deborah and I continued to eat artichokes and showed our pleasure in them. After a few such nights, one daughter became curious. Then, because *she* was curious, our other daughter had to try one. Now they get excited when artichoke hearts are on the dinner menu.

D: Showcasing a vegetable does require some thinking. Prepare your meal in terms of wetness and dryness. Serving Braised Artichokes (page 190) with a Cacciatora (page 157) might sound good in your head, but will surely result in two sauces combining in the middle of the plate. It's better to pair a sauced anything with Oven-Roasted Potatoes (page 193) or Sautéed Dandelion Greens with Garlic (page 182). And vice versa. Pollo al Mattone (page 143) hot off the grill would be much better paired with braised vegetables, offering a nice contrast of textures to boot.

G: And remember, when in doubt, if your vegetables are fresh, they're sometimes best sautéed or grilled with nothing more than salt, pepper, maybe a touch of lemon, and a drizzle of extra virgin olive oil.

SAUTÉED DANDELION GREENS
with garlic

CICORIA SALTATA

— SERVES 6 —

D: *When it comes to* cicoria, *the bitter, leafy, dark greens Italians love, the best way to enjoy them is to preserve their slight chewiness and sauté them quickly in olive oil and garlic. Dandelion greens are the closest thing we've found in America that has that kind of wild, delicious flavor, and maybe you even have some growing near you! Forage away and serve them with a Bistecca alla Fiorentina (page 140) and Oven-Roasted Potatoes (page 193). You'll be in for a treat.*

Kosher salt and freshly ground
    black pepper

2 bunches dandelion greens, Swiss chard,
    or Tuscan kale (aka lacinato, black
    kale, or cavolo nero), chopped into
    3-inch pieces

2 tablespoons extra virgin olive oil

3 garlic cloves, roughly chopped

Bring a large pot of water to a boil. Meanwhile, prepare an ice bath in a bowl. Add a pinch of salt and the greens to the boiling water. Cook for 2 to 3 minutes, until bright green. Using a spider, remove the greens and transfer them to the ice bath. When cooled, squeeze the excess water from the greens.

In a large skillet, heat the olive oil over medium-high heat until hot. Add the garlic and sauté for about 1 minute, until fragrant. Add the cooked greens and toss for 1 minute, or until warmed through.

Season with salt and pepper to taste and serve.

SAUTÉED ZUCCHINI

ZUCCHINI TRIFOLATI

SERVES 4–6

For Italians, the minimalist cooking style is perhaps best exemplified by the term trifolati, *which indicates something thinly sliced and sautéed with little interference: some olive oil, salt, and one fragrant touch, such as garlic or onion. Zucchini is an ideal trifolati candidate, especially a young zucchini with few seeds. And we suggest keeping your participation minimal. Don't even use a utensil to move the zucchini around in the pan: They'll break too easily. Use the handle to shake the pan a little and make the zucchini "jump."*

2 tablespoons extra virgin olive oil

6 small zucchini, halved lengthwise and cut crosswise into half-moons

½ small red onion, cut into thick chunks

Kosher salt and freshly ground black pepper

In a large nonstick skillet, heat the olive oil over medium-high heat until hot. Add the zucchini and onion and sauté for 10 to 12 minutes, until the zucchini is golden, almost charred.

Season with salt and pepper to taste and serve.

GRILLED MIXED VEGETABLES

VERDURE GRIGLIATA

· SERVES 6 ·

In Italy this is the side dish of summer—an array of freshly seared garden goodies that will give a barbecue main such as Florentine Steak (page 140) a rainbow of colors to liven the plate. Also, be sure to make enough to keep as leftovers in the fridge (they'll last another 4 or 5 days). They taste great in sandwiches, salads, and omelets, and can be added to a Red Sauce (page 55) for a vegetable-friendly pasta dish!

1 medium eggplant, thinly sliced

2 small zucchini, thinly sliced lengthwise

3 bell peppers (more than 1 color!), each cut into 8 pieces

1 red onion, quartered

Extra virgin olive oil, for drizzling

2 tablespoons roughly chopped fresh Italian parsley

Kosher salt and freshly ground black pepper

Preheat a grill to medium-high heat.

Grill the eggplant, zucchini, bell peppers, and onion for 3 to 5 minutes per side, depending on thickness. The vegetables should be soft and seared, but not mushy. Transfer to a platter and drizzle with olive oil. Garnish with parsley and season with salt and pepper to taste.

GRILLED ENDIVE
with gorgonzola and sage oil

INSALATA BELGA E GORGONZOLA

———————————— · SERVES 6–8 · ————————————

G: *A real joy of grilling season is serving up this elegant treat, which weds the smoky goodness of grilled endive with the strong flavors of melted Gorgonzola. These two don't overpower each other, although they will jockey for your taste buds' attention. The endive offers fabulous crunch, and the Gorgonzola serves up a sweet-and-sharp tang. It's a great balance, and the sage-infused olive oil helps bind them together. If you don't have a grill on hand, this dish can also be roasted in the oven.*

½ cup extra virgin olive oil

4 sprigs fresh sage

3 heads Belgian endive, halved lengthwise

4 ounces crumbled Gorgonzola

Kosher salt and freshly ground black pepper

Preheat a grill to high heat.

In a small saucepan, heat the olive oil until hot. Add the sage and cook for about 3 minutes to allow it to infuse the oil and until it becomes fragrant and slightly crispy. Remove from the heat.

Place the endive on the grill and grill for 4 minutes per side, until the leaves become lightly wilted and grill marks are prominent. Turn the endive cut-side up and top with the Gorgonzola. Close the grill lid and grill for 2 more minutes, until the cheese has softened.

Transfer the endive to a platter, drizzle with the sage-infused olive oil, season with salt and pepper to taste, and serve immediately.

FRIED ARTICHOKES

CARCIOFI FRITTI

————————————— • SERVES 6 • —————————————

D: *These crisp delights are an appetizer staple all over Italy, usually served in a cone of paper, to go with a great roasted meat dish. For a dream combination, we recommend these with the Roasted Pork Loin (page 152). This recipe calls for a quick dredging in flour before frying, but if you want an extra layer of mouthwatering crunch, try the beer batter mixture we use in our Fish Taco recipe (page 164).*

Juice of 1 lemon, plus 1 lemon, cut into 6 wedges, for serving

5 medium artichokes

1 cup all-purpose flour

1 teaspoon kosher salt, plus more for serving

¼ teaspoon freshly ground black pepper, plus more for serving

Vegetable oil, for frying

Fill a large bowl with water and add the lemon juice. Snap off the outer leaves from the artichokes until you reach the pale green leaves. Using a vegetable peeler, shave the stems to remove the woody outermost layer. Halve the artichokes lengthwise, through the stem. Using a spoon, remove the inedible hairy leaves (the chokes). Cut the artichokes into quarters. Place the artichokes in the lemon water to keep them from oxidizing and discoloring.

In a shallow dish, whisk together the flour, salt, and pepper.

In a high-sided skillet or Dutch oven, add the vegetable oil up to 2 inches, and heat over high heat until hot and smoking.

Dredge the artichokes in the seasoned flour, add to the hot oil, and fry for 4 to 5 minutes, flipping them occasionally with tongs, until golden and crisp. Transfer to a platter lined with paper towels to drain. Season with salt and serve warm with the lemon wedges.

BRAISED ARTICHOKES

CARCIOFI ALLA FIESOLANA

———— SERVES 4 ————

D: *I consider the artichoke romantic. It is a vegetable that has a journey to it, where you peel away layers to get to the heart. Here, Gabriele and I have modified the traditional Roman method of slow-cooking artichokes by using the baby kind. They require less cleaning, are more tender, and yield a perfectly edible choke. After they've been softened in the guanciale-infused oil and onion soffritto, you'll have a side dish to die for.*

Juice of 1 lemon

20 baby artichokes

1 cup vegetable stock, homemade (page 94)

3 tablespoons extra virgin olive oil

⅓ pound guanciale or pancetta, cut into ¼-inch cubes

1 red onion, finely diced

Kosher salt and freshly ground black pepper

1 handful fresh Italian parsley, finely chopped

Fill a large bowl with water and add the lemon juice. Snap off the outer leaves of each artichoke to uncover its pale green heart. Using a vegetable peeler, shave the stem of the artichoke until smooth. Using a knife, cut off the tip of the artichoke, as close as possible to the heart. Place each cleaned artichoke in the lemon water to prevent it from oxidizing and becoming discolored.

In a small pot, bring the stock to a simmer over medium-low heat. Reduce the heat to low and keep warm.

In a large nonstick skillet, heat the olive oil over medium-high heat until hot. Add the guanciale and sauté for 10 minutes, stirring often, until golden and crisp. Add the onion, reduce the heat to medium, and cook for about 5 minutes, until soft and translucent.

Reduce the heat to a simmer and place the artichoke hearts head down, one at a time, in the soffritto. Add a ladleful of warm vegetable stock and cover the pan. Cook for 40 to 50 minutes, or until very tender, adding a ladleful of stock as necessary as the liquid reduces and occasionally shaking the skillet gently to prevent the artichoke hearts from sticking to the surface. (You can also move them around with your fingers.)

Transfer to a platter, season with salt and pepper to taste, and sprinkle with the parsley. Serve immediately.

PEPPER AND POTATO STEW

PEPERONATA DI PATATE

G: *This is a real hunter's dish. All winter long you'll find this in Tuscan restaurants, especially on Sunday, because it would go perfectly with whatever was caught from that morning's hunt: pheasant, venison, rabbit. Those meats aren't always readily available in America, but this stew is a great accompaniment to grilled sausage or Pollo al Mattone (page 143).*

D: *The first time Gabriele made this for me, I couldn't believe how creamy it was, because the potatoes just melted into the peppers. It transcended every notion I'd had about sweet peppers.*

1 cup vegetable stock, homemade (page 94)

3 tablespoons extra virgin olive oil

1 small red onion, finely chopped

5 garlic cloves, cut into 3 chunks each

8 bell peppers (different colors), each cut into eighths

1 (15-ounce) can whole peeled tomatoes (pelati), puréed in a blender

1 pound russet (baking) potatoes, scrubbed well and cut into ½-inch cubes

Kosher salt and freshly ground black pepper

1 handful fresh Italian parsley, roughly chopped

In a small pot, heat the stock over medium-low heat until just before boiling. Reduce the heat to low and keep warm.

In a large Dutch oven, heat the olive oil over medium-high heat until hot. Add the onion and sauté for 5 to 7 minutes, or until completely softened but not browned. Add the garlic and sauté for an additional 2 minutes, until fragrant but not browned.

Add the bell peppers, reduce the heat to medium-low, stir, partially cover, and cook for 10 minutes, until softened.

Add the tomatoes and potatoes, season with salt and pepper to taste, stir well, and cook for about 1 hour, occasionally adding a ladleful of vegetable stock as needed to keep the ingredients cooking. The resulting stew should have a thick consistency. To check for doneness, using a wooden spoon, isolate one piece of potato and press it against the side of the pot. If it doesn't offer any resistance as it mashes, the stew is ready to serve.

Stir in the parsley and serve.

OVEN-ROASTED POTATOES

PATATE ARROSTO

D: *When these roasted beauties reach that stage where they're caramelized on the outside and soft on the inside, you have achieved the perfect side dish. The Yukon Golds can also be parboiled whole and sautéed on the stovetop (see note), in which case the serving time is more forgiving than in an oven. Roasting in an oven really affects a potato chunk's texture in such a way that the potatoes need to be served immediately, otherwise they'll dry out.*

6 Yukon Gold potatoes, cut into ¾-inch cubes

4 carrots, halved lengthwise and cut into chunks

5 garlic cloves

1 handful fresh rosemary sprigs

1 handful sage leaves

¼ cup extra virgin olive oil

Kosher salt and freshly ground black pepper

Preheat the oven to 400°F.

On a baking sheet, place the potatoes, carrots, garlic, rosemary, and sage. Drizzle with the olive oil, season with salt and pepper to taste, and toss to coat.

Roast for 50 to 60 minutes, tossing halfway through, until the potatoes are crisp and golden. Remove from the oven and serve.

IMPORTANTE! To parboil and pan-roast these potatoes: In a pot, combine the whole potatoes with water to cover. Bring to a boil and cook for 15 minutes. Remove the potatoes from the pot and set them aside to cool. Cut the potatoes into ¾-inch chunks and add to a large nonstick skillet with the carrots, garlic, rosemary, and sage. Dress with olive oil, salt, and pepper, and heat on high until the potatoes are crisp and golden, occasionally moving the potatoes by shaking the pan handle. Avoid stirring with a spoon or spatula, so that you don't break the skin, and the potatoes can achieve a nice sear.

EGGPLANT PARMESAN

MELANZANE ALLA PARMIGIANA

D: *This is one of our favorite dishes. It is so beloved in our family that it's our New Year's Eve dinner staple at home. But instead of the smothered-in-sauce-and-cheese version you regularly find in restaurants, ours boasts carefully balanced layers of tomato sauce, mozzarella, and eggplant, and it leaves out the ricotta. Our recipe is a valentine to that meaty purple eggplant, which has a fascinating history: it's been called everything from an aphrodisiac (a "love apple") to a cause of insanity. We are mad for our eggplant Parmesan, which is intended as an entree, though light enough to moonlight as a side dish. But it takes some planning and patience, so when you dig in to the making of it, whip up a few batches!*

Canola oil, for frying

1 cup all-purpose flour

1 teaspoon sea salt

¼ teaspoon freshly ground black pepper

3 medium eggplants, cut into ¼-inch-thick slices

4 cups Red Sauce (page 55)

¾ pound part-skim mozzarella cheese, freshly shredded

1 cup freshly grated Parmigiano-Reggiano cheese, plus more for serving

1½ cups fresh basil leaves, plus more for garnish

Extra virgin olive oil, for serving

Preheat the oven to 400°F.

In a large, heavy-bottomed pot or high-sided skillet, pour in 2 inches of canola oil. Heat over high heat until a deep-fry thermometer reads 360°F. (You can also test by adding a small piece of bread to the oil. If it fries and browns, the oil is ready.)

In a shallow dish, whisk together the flour, salt, and pepper. Working in batches of approximately 8 slices each, dredge the eggplant slices in the flour mixture and add them to the hot oil. Fry for 1 to 2 minutes each, until browned. Using tongs, transfer the eggplant to a baking sheet lined with paper towels to let cool.

In two 13 × 9-inch baking dishes, place one layer of eggplant slices. Brush each with a thin layer of Red Sauce, top with a layer of mozzarella, 2 tablespoons Parmesan, and a sprinkle of basil leaves. Repeat the layering two more times. Make a final layer of Red Sauce, mozzarella, and Parmesan.

Bake for 25 to 30 minutes, until bubbling and golden on top. Garnish with a final sprinkling of basil leaves and Parmesan, and a small drizzle of olive oil.

pizza

G: Pizza-making is a very particular food memory for me. I was twelve years old when my parents tapped me to make all the pizzas for my mother's fortieth birthday party. For six hours I sweated in front of our family's big fireplace— a table full of ingredients for toppings in front of me—and made around seventy pizzas. They gave me the equivalent of one hundred dollars, and let me tell you, it was earned.

D: No tips from your mother's friends?

G: Well, yes, many of them were generous. I put a little showmanship into it. It was certainly a more fun way to earn money than pushing a lawnmower up the hills of our property.

D: And even more fun than making them is eating them, but we definitely get fun out of making pizza at home with our kids. When we have pizza night, it's as if a map of dough has been laid out, and everyone stakes their claim before it goes into the oven. "I want mushrooms!" "I want tomatoes and mozzarella!" "I want arugula and prosciutto!" Then the pizza comes out, the countries get divided, and everyone's happy. World peace at the dinner table!

G: Pizza gets such a bad rap as junk food, when really it's a wonderful delivery system for fresh ingredients. When you take control of making pizza at home, you can avoid the doughy, oily, meat-laden, and heavily cheesed pies from so many chain delivery places. Making thin-crust pizzas with fresh toppings of your choice leads to a much healthier and tastier experience.

D: Experiment with flavors, too. It's how we came up with our Breakfast Pizza (page 205). There's very little that doesn't taste good on baked pizza dough. But remember, although we offer a foolproof recipe for great Pizza Dough (page 201), you can also buy it at your local grocery store, pizza shop, or neighborhood baker.

G: If you have a wood-burning oven: Rotate the pizza a few times with the pizza peel while it cooks, since the fire is on one side of the oven. Otherwise, the pizza will cook unevenly. If you are using a pizza stone: Make sure it's preheated—for a good hour at your oven's highest temperature—before you bake. If your pizza sticks, it usually means the stone wasn't preheated enough.

PIZZA DOUGH

IMPASTO

———————————————— MAKES 4 ————————————————

G: *There's nothing like the feeling of using your hands to make something that you know will be thoroughly enjoyed later. This recipe comes from Carlo Polpini, a friend of my father's who was a famous pizza maker in Florence. It's simple, easy to follow, and works wonderfully, and I've been using it ever since I started making pizzas with my father when I was a child. During the rising process, be sure not to let the dough rise too much, otherwise the top will get a little dry and crusty. Kids like to help make this.*

1 (¼-ounce) envelope active dry yeast (2¼ teaspoons)

½ cup lukewarm water (approximately 80°F)

4 cups bread flour

1½ teaspoons salt

¼ cup extra virgin olive oil, plus more for greasing

All-purpose flour, for dusting

In a stand mixer fitted with the dough hook, combine the yeast, lukewarm water, and ½ cup of the bread flour. Mix well and let it sit for 30 minutes, or until bubbly, like foamy beer.

In a separate medium bowl, whisk together the remaining 3½ cups bread flour and the salt until evenly combined.

Add ¾ cup cold water and the olive oil to the yeast mixture. Turn on the mixer and begin adding the flour mixture in increments, then mix for 5 minutes, until the dough starts creeping up the dough hook and detaching from the sides of the bowl.

Grease a large bowl with oil and transfer the dough to the bowl. Turn the dough to coat its surface with oil. Cover the bowl loosely with a tea towel. Let the dough rise until doubled in size, about 2 hours. Punch the dough down, then let rise another 1 hour.

Divide the dough into 4 equal pieces and form into discs. On a work surface lightly dusted with flour, use your fingers or the heel of your hand (and a rolling pin, if you prefer) to stretch the discs until they're 13 inches in diameter. The disc should be very thin, less than ⅛ inch.

IMPORTANTE! If you're making pizza within the hour after forming the pizza dough discs, they can be kept at room temperature. Otherwise, place them on a baking sheet, cover with plastic wrap, and refrigerate for up to 12 hours before baking, as long as the dough doesn't rise too much, because acidity will creep in and the flavor will sour. Ideally, though, you should make the pizzas the same day you make the dough.

TOMATO, ANCHOVY, AND CAPER PIZZA

PIZZA NAPOLETANA

———— SERVES 4 ————

G: *This homage to Naples, where pizza was born, gets its salty, bold kick from anchovies and capers. It's my father's absolute favorite. This recipe includes oregano, which is a seasoning I'm not wild about, so if you're like me, you can leave it off.*

Pizza Dough (page 201), formed into 4 (13-inch) discs, at room temperature

1 cup canned whole peeled tomatoes (pelati), puréed in a blender

Salt and freshly ground black pepper

16 anchovy fillets, slivered

1 teaspoon fresh oregano

1 tablespoon capers, rinsed

Extra virgin olive oil, for drizzling

Place a pizza stone in the oven and preheat to 500°F for 1 hour before baking. (Or preheat a wood-fired pizza oven to very hot, 4 hours before baking.)

Using a spoon, spread one-fourth of the puréed tomatoes on 1 disc of dough, leaving a 1-inch border all around. Season with salt and pepper to taste. Sprinkle with one-fourth of the anchovies, oregano, and capers.

Gently place the pizza on the pizza stone and bake for about 5 minutes, until golden with slight signs of charring. (If using a wood-fired oven, gently place the pizza on the oven floor, and bake for 3 minutes, or until golden and crisp.)

Remove the pizza from the oven and transfer to a cutting board. Drizzle with the olive oil, slice, and serve immediately.

Repeat with the remaining 3 pizza discs.

TOMATO, MOZZARELLA, AND BASIL PIZZA

PIZZA MARGHERITA

· SERVES 4 ·

D: *I love that pizza Margherita was developed by a Neapolitan cook in the nineteenth century to serve his queen. And impress her it did, since he slyly and simply highlighted the colors of the Italian flag in the pizza: red (tomatoes), white (mozzarella), and green (basil)! This is the prototype pizza, the go-to classic that kids love. When you say "pizza" in Gabriele's homeland, this is what comes to mind, and rightly so. With fresh ingredients, it practically transports you to Italy.*

1 cup canned whole peeled tomatoes (pelati)

Kosher salt and freshly ground black pepper

Pizza Dough (page 201), formed into 4 (13-inch) discs, at room temperature

½ pound mozzarella cheese, shredded

1 handful fresh basil leaves

Extra virgin olive oil, for drizzling

Place a pizza stone in the oven and preheat to 500°F for 1 hour before baking. (Or preheat a wood-fired pizza oven to very hot, 4 hours before baking.)

In a food processor, purée the tomatoes until smooth. Season with salt and pepper to taste. Using a spoon, spread one-fourth of the tomato sauce on 1 disc of dough, leaving a 1-inch border all around. Sprinkle with one-fourth of the mozzarella.

Gently place the pizza on the pizza stone and bake for about 5 minutes, until golden with slight signs of charring. (If using a wood-fired oven, gently place the pizza on the oven floor, and bake for 3 minutes, or until golden and crisp.)

Remove the pizza from the oven and transfer to a cutting board. Slice, garnish with basil and a drizzle of olive oil, and serve immediately.

Repeat with the remaining 3 pizza discs.

BUFFALO MOZZARELLA AND HEIRLOOM TOMATO PIZZA

MOZZARELLA DI BUFALA E POMODORI

SERVES 4

D: *Tomato sauce on pizza can taste great, and using fresh tomato slices can be spectacular. Paired with milky fresh buffalo mozzarella, this pizza is closer to the pleasure one gets from a bruschetta. A pizza like this is proof that when done right, pizza is hardly something to feel guilty about!*

14 ounces buffalo mozzarella cheese, shredded

Pizza Dough (page 201), formed into 4 (13-inch) discs, at room temperature

2 heirloom tomatoes, cut into 20 to 24 (¼-inch-thick) slices

Salt and freshly ground black pepper

½ cup fresh basil leaves

Extra virgin olive oil, for drizzling

Place a pizza stone in the oven and preheat to 500°F for 1 hour before baking. (Or preheat a wood-fired pizza oven to very hot, 4 hours before baking.)

Sprinkle one-fourth of the mozzarella on 1 disc of dough, leaving a 1-inch border all around. Top with 5 to 6 tomato slices. Season with salt and pepper to taste.

Gently place the pizza on the pizza stone and bake for about 5 minutes, until golden with slight signs of charring. (If using a wood-fired oven, gently place the pizza on the oven floor, and bake for 3 minutes, or until golden and crisp.)

Remove the pizza from the oven, transfer to a cutting board, and garnish with a few basil leaves and a drizzle of olive oil. Slice and serve immediately.

Repeat with the remaining 3 pizza discs.

BREAKFAST PIZZA

PIZZA A COLAZIONE

(pictured on pages 196–197)

———————————— • SERVES 4 • ————————————

D: *One day friends were coming over for lunch, so we got the wood-fired pizza oven started. Earlier that day, when we were still in our bathrobes, you had this idea.*

G: *The oven was hot, we were hungry, we had fresh eggs from our chickens, and the pizza dough was already made. So the thought of a breakfast pizza materialized.*

D: *The concept is simple and inspired: eggs and bacon—in this case, pancetta—but on a tomato-and-cheese pizza. It was so delicious.*

G: *It's so much fun to crack that egg over the pizza and let the heat of the oven cook it. It works just as well in a kitchen oven. So the next time a weekend rolls around, skip the same-old breakfast, and try this variation.*

1 cup canned whole peeled tomatoes (pelati)

Kosher salt

2 tablespoons extra virgin olive oil

¼ pound pancetta, diced medium

Pizza Dough (page 201), formed into 4 (13-inch) discs, at room temperature

½ pound mozzarella cheese, shredded

4 large eggs

1 handful fresh basil leaves

Place a pizza stone in the oven and preheat to 500°F for 1 hour before baking. (Or preheat a wood-fired pizza oven to very hot, 4 hours before baking.)

In a food processor, purée the tomatoes until smooth. Season with salt to taste.

In a skillet, heat the olive oil and pancetta over medium heat and cook for 5 to 7 minutes, or until crisp.

Using a spoon, spread one-fourth of the puréed tomatoes on 1 disc of dough, leaving a 1-inch border all around. Sprinkle one-fourth of the mozzarella on top.

Gently place the pizza on the pizza stone and bake for about 5 minutes, until golden with slight signs of charring. (If using a wood-fired oven, gently place the pizza on the oven floor, and bake for 3 minutes, or until golden and crisp.)

Remove the pizza from the oven and break an egg over the center of the pizza. Top with one-fourth of the cooked pancetta, return the pizza to the oven, and bake another 3 to 4 minutes (1 to 2 minutes if using a wood-fired oven), until the egg is cooked.

Remove the pizza from the oven, transfer to a cutting board, and top with one-fourth of the basil. Serve immediately. Repeat with the remaining 3 pizza discs.

WHITE PIZZA
with prosciutto and arugula

PIZZA BIANCA CON PROSCIUTTO E RUCOLA

— SERVES 4 —

D: *Who said pizza had to have tomatoes? This alternative might very well turn you into a pizza bianca fan. The key is that you're using prosciutto and fresh arugula as a topping untouched by oven heat. Once the cheese is melted, pull it out of the oven, add the cured meat and peppery arugula, and enjoy, perhaps with a cold one!*

½ **pound mozzarella cheese, shredded**

Pizza Dough (page 201), formed into 4 (13-inch) discs, at room temperature

⅓ **pound prosciutto, thinly sliced**

4 handfuls arugula

Extra virgin olive oil, for drizzling

Kosher salt and freshly ground black pepper

Place a pizza stone in the oven and preheat to 500°F for 1 hour before baking. (Or preheat a wood-fired pizza oven to very hot, 4 hours before baking.)

Sprinkle one-fourth of the cheese on 1 disc of dough, leaving a 1-inch border all around. Gently place the pizza on the pizza stone and bake for about 5 minutes, until golden with slight signs of charring. (If using a wood-fired oven, gently place the pizza on the oven floor, and bake for 3 minutes, or until golden and crisp.)

Remove the pizza from the oven, transfer to a cutting board, and top with one-fourth of the prosciutto and 1 handful of the arugula. Drizzle with olive oil and season with salt and pepper. Slice and serve immediately.

Repeat with the remaining 3 pizza discs.

RAW BEEF PIZZA

PIZZA AL CARPACCIO

· SERVES 4 ·

G: *When I was asked to develop a dish to serve at the Meatopia Festival in New York, the thought of going bold with beef and pizza led to this inspiration. We used eye of round from certified Piedmontese steer and, from a truck with a mounted pizza oven, we presented carpaccio on baked pizza dough. With a thin, nicely charred crust, fresh rosemary, nutty arugula, and quality beef with a squeeze of lemon, it's out-of-this-world good! If you feel like splurging—and we couldn't that day, since we had to serve 3,000 people—use filet mignon.*

1½ pounds eye of round, trimmed of fat and sinew, chilled for 10 minutes in the freezer

Extra virgin olive oil, for drizzling

Pizza Dough (page 201), formed into 4 (13-inch) discs, at room temperature

Sea salt and freshly ground black pepper

Leaves from 3 sprigs fresh rosemary

4 ounces baby arugula

5 lemons, each cut into 8 wedges

Place a pizza stone in the oven and preheat to 500°F for 1 hour before baking. (Or preheat a wood-fired pizza oven to very hot, 4 hours before baking.)

One hour before baking, using a very sharp knife, thinly slice the beef against the grain, until you have about 40 slices. (You could also have a butcher do this for you, but you'd need to come home and prepare this immediately so it doesn't discolor.) Place the carpaccio slices in 1 layer on wax paper and refrigerate until ready to use.

Drizzle olive oil on 1 disc of dough, season with salt and pepper to taste, and sprinkle one-fourth of the rosemary on top. Gently place the pizza on the pizza stone and bake for about 5 minutes, until golden with slight signs of charring. (If using a wood-fired oven, gently place the pizza on the oven floor, and bake for 3 minutes, or until golden and crisp.)

Remove the pizza from the oven, set aside to cool, and repeat with the remaining 3 pizza discs.

Transfer the pizzas to a cutting board, and slice each into 8 to 10 slices . Lay 1 or 2 slices of carpaccio over each slice, sprinkle with arugula, and serve with a lemon wedge.

IMPORTANTE! If you're hand-slicing the carpaccio yourself, supreme thinness is the key. But if your slices still aren't thin enough, lay them flat on a board, cover with plastic wrap, and pound them lightly with a meat tenderizer (or wine bottle bottom) to flatten.

panini

G : In Italy, sandwiches are the great portable food, a supremely fulfilling way to enjoy freshly baked bread and delicious ingredients in practically any setting: a picnic, a day at the beach, a ride into the countryside, or a lunch with friends in the backyard. With so many different kinds of cheeses, vegetables, and cold cuts, there's a seemingly endless array of flavors for mixing and matching. My mother would even send us to school with a frittata between slices of bread! I loved it, because by mid-morning the frittata's butteriness had soaked into the bread, which meant the outside was crispy, while the eggy filling was the right amount of soggy. For a kosher kid without a cured pig sandwich option, this was a highly enjoyable alternative.

Panini in Italy aren't always grilled (as many Americans have come to assume from the popularity of the pressed kind), but what they should always be are delicious. It's a point of pride for Italians who work in an office to head to the best local deli and order the freshly baked ciabatta spread with truffle-infused butter, layered with porcini mushrooms sautéed with mint, and topped with a few slices of speck. Or they grab a clean, simple, mortadella-and-bread combo—no extras—and wash it down with a glass of Moretti beer. (And there are probably hearty sandwich lovers who get both!) In Italy, a well-thought-out *panino*—never overstuffed but filled with the best ingredients—reflects your personality.

For me, a great *panino* often starts with bread I've made myself. Making bread gives meaning to my day. It means a beautiful loaf to have with dinner, followed by toast the next morning , then that mouthwatering *panino* for lunch. If there's any left over, I let it get stale to give heft to a soup or become croutons in a salad. That cycle goes straight to the essence of the joy I get from feeding my family. It's a daily activity I wholeheartedly recommend mastering, because there are few household aromas as wonderful as a freshly baked loaf of bread reaching its full potential in your oven.

Deborah and our daughters can tell you how obsessed I became when I decided to master the process of baking bread. I tried every kind of flour, yeast, and dough hydration. Longer rising times, shorter rising times. Wetter dough, drier dough. I knew the taste I wanted: a very lightly salted loaf of rustic goodness, with a dark crust crunch that nicely offsets the pillowy consistency inside. But getting an Italian to spell out a recipe for me wasn't so easy. I asked our local baker in Italy: "How do you make your bread?" The baker: "Some water, some flour, some yeast." Me: "Um, proportions?" The baker: "What?" Later, me to my grandmother: "Nonna, how did you make bread when we were little?" Nonna: "Oh, some water, some flour, some yeast." Me: [*Sigh.*]

Eventually I found inspiration from other bakers, but it was learning about the use of a heated cast iron pot as a de facto bread oven for the initial baking process that proved revelatory. I also hit upon a way to keep rising dough from temperature inconsistencies in the kitchen, like an open window, or a door that keeps opening and closing. One day I pulled my pizza stone out of the oven—I always keep it there—and noticed that it was slightly warmer than room temperature. I realized the oven light had been on the whole time, and had been gently heating up the oven. Guess where my dough rises now?

In the oven, with the light on. The temperature will eventually reach anywhere between 70° and 75°F (depending on the oven) and there won't be any drafts to alter the rising time!

When you start making bread, also think about your schedule. When do you want it freshest? In the morning? Afternoon? Right before dinner? Once you have a good idea how long it takes to make your optimum bread, put yourself on a schedule to start the process so it's ready when you want it. As I mentioned earlier, it helps keep me on schedule. I know when I have time to do all the other things in the day that need to get done: picking up the kids, running errands, arranging a meeting. In some ways, making bread is like having an extra baby in the house you have to take care of—it'll bring out your nurturing side.

As for the finished product, farmers in Tuscany believe good bread needs to rest for a day, so the gluten can relax, the crust can achieve its ideal crunch, and the inside can reach a premium texture. It can be difficult to resist cutting into a warm loaf when that special aroma pervades the kitchen. But if you slide a knife through it, the dough might still be a little sticky inside and start compressing. Then you'll be changing the shape of your bread before it's had time to cool, get settled, and release some moisture. If you don't want to wait until the next day, give it at least an extra 30 to 45 minutes of rest. If you wait overnight though, you can embrace the traditional saying in Tuscany about a farmer's food calendar: *L'uovo di oggi, il pane di ieri, ed il vino dell'anno scorso.* "The egg from today, the bread from yesterday, and the wine from last year."

Happy baking and panini-making!

BREAD STARTER

G: *The starter is a mixture of water, flour, and yeast that, when fermented, allows bread to rise. Though it's popular to use an active dry yeast to kickstart the fermentation process, I like to rely on natural yeast that colonizes the water-flour mixture. It's that extra poetic touch I like about breadmaking, in that you're allowing the environment to create something. Since whole wheat flour, less refined than white, attracts more natural bacteria, I recommend using a flour mixture of 50 percent Italian 00 flour and 50 percent whole wheat flour when making a first starter. Once the starter is ready and healthy, I then feed it exclusively white flour. Remember, when starting from scratch, it takes anywhere from 1 week to 10 days to develop a starter, depending on factors such as the temperature of your kitchen. (The higher the temperature, the faster the fermentation.) Once you have your starter, as long as you keep it fed—and I've occasionally assigned starter-babysitting duties to Deborah if work takes me out of town—the ability to make bread will always be at your fingertips. Also, you'll need a digital kitchen scale for weighing out your ingredients, as well as those in other baking recipes like Chestnut Flour Cake (page 233), so buy yourself an inexpensive one.*

50 grams water, plus more for feeding the starter

50 grams whole wheat flour

All-purpose flour, for feeding the starter

In a 2-cup container, combine the water and whole wheat flour and stir well. Let it sit in a cool, shaded area of the kitchen for at least 2 days.

On the third day, discard 80 percent of the mixture and replenish with equal amounts of all-purpose flour and water. This is called "feeding." (If beginning with more than 100 grams of flour and water, a good discarding rule is to save about 2 tablespoons of starter per 100-gram mixture.)

Feed the starter every day after that. By the fourth or fifth day, look for small air bubbles on the surface. At the end of each 24-hour cycle after that, the scent of the starter will change from its initial creamy, buttery overtones to distinctly vinegary, once the fermentation process has occurred.

By the end of the first week, with regular feeding at the same time each day, the starter will have reached an especially lively, predictable rhythm cycle of culture-forming and decay. Your adventures in bread making can begin!

Twelve hours before you plan to make bread dough—preferably the evening before creating a dough in the morning—discard 80 percent of the starter, replenish with 100 grams water and 100 grams all-purpose flour, and mix well. This will become the starter you use to make Pane Toscano (page 216).

IMPORTANTE! Once a starter is alive and healthy, it can be frozen up to 3 months in a hard plastic container with a perforated lid. Once thawed at room temperature, the starter will need 2 to 3 days to get back into rising-and-feeding shape before you can bake with it.

TUSCAN BREAD

PANE TOSCANO

———————————————————— MAKES 1 LOAF ————————————————————

G: *Tuscan bread doesn't have salt! Origin stories vary: One legend attributes it to how expensive salt became during the economically depressed Middle Ages. Another theory—which appeals to my fighting spirit as a Tuscan—involves the ancient rivalry between coastal Pisa and inland Florence, and how Pisa tried to punish Florentines by halting the transportation of salt from the shore. The Florentines decided that their food was so good, salt was superfluous.*

The culinary reality, however, is true, in that Tuscan food is so flavorful already, due to fresh ingredients and wonderful herbs, that the bread really didn't need salt. If you must have that bread bite before the pasta arrives, a drizzle of high-quality extra virgin olive oil and a pinch of salt—both readily available at any Tuscan tavola *(table)—will offer plenty of flavor. But if you wait until you have sauce to soak, that's when you'll find the best use for our saltless bread.*

To make a pane Pugliese (named after the Puglia region in the boot of Italy, known for their rustic, hearty breads), the adjustment is simple. Just add . . . salt!

350 grams warm water (80° to 85°F)

120 grams Bread Starter (page 214) or mother dough

500 grams bread flour, plus more for dusting and coating

7 grams salt (for pane Pugliese; optional)

In a large bowl, combine the warm water and starter and, using your hands, break down the starter until the excess water is absorbed completely into the dough.

Add the flour and mix with your hands until a dough forms and there are no lumps. The dough should feel elastic and slightly wet. (If making Pugliese bread, add the salt now and mix well.) Transfer the dough to a plastic container and cover with a cloth. (If you're working with a mother dough, which is a saved piece of the previous day's bread dough, remove approximately 120 grams and set it aside in a partially ventilated plastic container. This will be the starter the following day.)

Every 30 minutes, for 2 hours, wet your hands and gently pull the dough away from the sides of the container, toward you, then fold it back inside the container. Let the dough sit for 3 hours, after which the first rise will be complete, and the dough should have grown by one-third to one-half its original volume.

Transfer the dough to a work surface lightly dusted with flour. Using a bench knife

(continued)

(also known as a dough scraper), mold the dough into a round shape and let it rest for 30 minutes. The dough will relax and look like a deflated ball at this point.

Coat a round, lined proofing basket—called a banetton—with bread flour, or, if using a brand new banetton, a flour mix of 70 percent bread flour and 30 percent semolina. (Semolina flour is very grainy and dry, and it will help prevent the dough from sticking to the sides.)

With the bench knife, flip the dough, then stretch it to about 3 times its original length. Fold it back to its original size, roll it lightly in your hands, and place it in the banetton. Cover with a kitchen towel and let it rise undisturbed in a warm spot for 3 hours. (An oven with its interior light turned on works quite well, protecting the dough from sudden temperature changes.)

Place a pizza stone and 5-quart cast iron Dutch oven in the oven, and preheat the oven to 500°F. Once the temperature has been reached, let the pot sit in the oven for 30 minutes longer.

Place a sheet of parchment paper over the banetton, place a pizza peel on top, and gently turn upside down. Carefully remove the banetton to uncover the bread, which should now be resting on the parchment paper–lined pizza peel. Be careful not to rip any potentially sticking dough, especially if using a new banetton. (Ripped dough won't rise properly in the oven.)

Using a very sharp knife, make 2 or 3 short cuts in the dough along the white flour lines left on the dough by the sides of the banetton.

Gently slide the parchment paper with the dough onto the pizza stone and cover with the overturned cast iron pot. Reduce the temperature to 450°F. (All ovens are different, so after a trial run, you may determine the heat needs to be higher.)

Bake for 30 minutes. Remove the cast iron pot. The loaf should be golden in color, with a smattering of dark edges. Bake an additional 20 minutes uncovered, moving the bread occasionally to ensure the loaf bakes evenly on all sides, until the crust looks lightly toasted in color, with a slightly blistered appearance.

Remove the bread from the oven and cool on a wire rack, uncovered, for at least 1 hour.

IMPORTANTE! When winter hits, the temperature drop really starts to affect the quality of bread rising. So I add another 3 tablespoons warm water, ¼ teaspoon sugar, and ¼ teaspoon active dry yeast to the initial mixture of warmed water and starter, and let it act as a stabilizer for this recipe. It helps the bread resist and survive those microclimate changes. In extreme heat, that trick is not necessary, especially if your bread starter is strong.

HEIRLOOM TOMATO AND MOZZARELLA SANDWICH
with basil oil

CAPRESE

───────────────────── · SERVES 4 · ─────────────────────

D: *When we're spending time outdoors with the kids during the summer and we want something fresh, light, and flavorful, this sandwich does the trick. Pack the baguette, tomatoes, and mozzarella separately, and you can easily assemble it on the spot so it doesn't get soggy. Our basil oil is a beautiful dressing, too, and a way to infuse the taste of basil into the bread. Happy picnicking!*

2 heirloom tomatoes, cut into 12 slices

Kosher salt

1 large baguette, at least 24 inches long, split lengthwise

3 balls (about 1 pound) fresh mozzarella cheese, thickly sliced

8 fresh basil leaves

Basil Oil (recipe follows), for drizzling

Season the tomatoes with salt, and layer them on the inside of the baguette. Add a layer using all of the mozzarella slices, and top with the basil leaves.

Drizzle with the basil oil and close the baguette. Slice crosswise into 4 sandwiches.

BASIL OIL
MAKES 1 CUP

Leaves from 2 bunches fresh basil

1 cup extra virgin olive oil

Kosher salt and freshly ground black pepper

Juice of 1 lemon

Bring a small pot of water to a boil. Set up a bowl with an ice bath. Add the basil leaves to the boiling water and cook for 45 seconds to 1 minute, until lightly softened. Transfer immediately to the ice bath to prevent further cooking. Drain and let dry.

In a blender, combine the basil and olive oil and blend until smooth. Strain through a strainer lined with cheesecloth into a medium bowl.

Season with salt and pepper to taste. Add the lemon juice right before serving.

GRILLED MOZZARELLA SANDWICH

MOZZARELLA IN CARROZZA

SERVES 4

G: *This is the Tuscan version of grilled cheese, which my dad often made for me when I was a kid. There's real pleasure in an eggy sandwich, fried in a way that seals in melted mozzarella. This warm, rustic* panino *is so beloved where I'm from that you can find it on most restaurant menus in Florence, plated as if it were no less meal-worthy than a bowl of pasta or meat dish.*

¾ pound buffalo mozzarella cheese, cut into ¾-inch-thick slices

8 slices Pane Toscano (page 216), or soft white bread

3 large eggs

½ cup whole milk

Salt and freshly ground black pepper

3 tablespoons extra virgin olive oil

½ cup all-purpose flour, for dusting

Lay one-fourth of the mozzarella between 2 slices of bread and close. Repeat with the remaining bread slices.

In a small shallow baking dish, whisk together the eggs and milk. Season with salt and pepper to taste.

Meanwhile, in a large nonstick skillet, heat the olive oil over medium-high heat until hot. Dust 1 sandwich with flour, dip it in the egg mixture, then add it to the pan. Fry about 3 minutes on each side, until the outside is golden and crisp, but not burned, and the mozzarella is completely melted.

Remove the sandwich from the pan, then repeat with the other 3 sandwiches.

Cut each sandwich in half and serve.

SPECK, PECORINO, AND GRILLED EGGPLANT SANDWICH

ZINGARATA CON PANINO

— SERVES 4 —

G: *The term* zingarata *refers to a carefree car trip out of town with a group of friends, an excursion that might lead you into unexpected adventures. That's how I see this* panino, *a rich merging of flavors one might not think to combine—smoky cured meat, wonderfully salty Pecorino, and summery eggplant. It's a hearty mouthful that will transport you.*

1 small eggplant, cut crosswise into 12 thin slices

1 garlic clove, minced

1 tablespoon finely chopped fresh Italian parsley

3 tablespoons extra virgin olive oil

Salt and freshly ground black pepper

4 (4-inch-wide) slices ciabatta, split lengthwise

¼ pound young Pecorino Toscano cheese, cut into 12 slices

12 slices speck

Heat a grill pan over medium-high heat. Add the eggplant and grill for 2 to 3 minutes per side, until grill-marked and softened. Remove from the heat and transfer to a medium bowl.

To the eggplant bowl, add the garlic, parsley, olive oil, and salt and pepper to taste and toss until the eggplant is well coated.

Layer the bottom half of each ciabatta piece with 3 slices Pecorino, 3 slices speck, and 3 slices eggplant. Close each sandwich and press firmly.

SOPPRESSATA AND MARINATED ARTICHOKE SANDWICH

SOPPRESSATA E CARCIOFINI PANINO

────────────────────────────── SERVES 3 ──────────────────────────────

D: *If you have some quality marinated artichokes, preferably the kind simply marinated in olive oil, this* panino *delivers a punch. Soppressata is a beautifully rustic, richly flavored dry salami that has been enjoyed over the years by nobles and peasants alike. With the marinated artichokes, and a soft, young Pecorino, this is sandwich gold.*

Extra virgin olive oil, for drizzling

6 slices Pane Toscano (page 216) or Pugliese bread

Sea salt and freshly ground black pepper

9 slices soppressata

9 slices young Pecorino (like Cacio di Roma) or Provolone

3 marinated artichokes, thinly sliced

Drizzle olive oil over the 6 slices of bread and season with salt and pepper to taste.

On each of 3 slices of bread, lay 3 slices soppressata, 3 slices Pecorino, and 1 sliced artichoke. Close the sandwiches with the remaining bread slices and serve.

PROSCIUTTO AND TALEGGIO SANDWICH

with fig preserves

PROSCIUTTO FORMAGGIO E MARMELLATA PANINO

· SERVES 2 ·

D: *Salty and creamy, tart and sweet, cool and hot, this sandwich is sexy. If you press it in the heated pan until it's just barely warm and melty, you'll be rewarded with a bite that yields the best flavor from all the ingredients. You'll start wondering why fig preserves can't be in everything you make from now on.*

2 (4-inch-wide) slices ciabatta, split lengthwise

2 tablespoons fig or apricot preserves

¼ pound Taleggio cheese, sliced

6 slices prosciutto

½ cup thinly sliced radicchio

Extra virgin olive oil, for brushing

Heat a medium cast iron skillet or grill pan over medium heat.

Spread the bottom half of each ciabatta piece with 1 tablespoon fig preserves. Top with one-half of the Taleggio, prosciutto, and radicchio. Close with the top slice of bread and brush the outside of the sandwich with the olive oil.

Place each sandwich in the pan and press with a flat, heavy lid or sandwich press until the cheese is just melted.

Remove from the heat, slice in half, and serve.

DATE NIGHT

With kids, our routine of home life is as busy as a beehive, with all energies usually directed toward them. Getting the children to school, picking them up, scheduling their activities, arranging their play dates, transporting them here and there, and, of course, feeding them well.

That doesn't always leave a lot of alone time for us, however. And sometimes when that alone time presents itself, we're simply too exhausted to take advantage of it!

We love our special date nights, planned so meticulously, with the night split in two—making something simple for the children, then enjoying a more sophisticated and intimate dinner for us after they go to bed.

It does require a bit of a night-owl mentality to begin eating a meal as late as eleven o'clock. But when we're set up in advance, the anticipation of quality time is enough to keep us awake. Plus, there's always espresso.

What we like to do is, first and foremost, make a meal plan. The idea is to feed the kids something that keeps their mood light and happy, so that they might—fingers crossed!—be amenable to going to bed early. This is a great time to pull out leftovers. If there's Red Sauce (page 55) or Pesto (page 63) available, spaghetti's an easy choice. Above all, we're looking for a smooth evening, since we're planning two dinners. If we're having a pasta dish, we'll make sure that when the kids finally hit the hay, all that's left to do is boil the pasta. The sauce will have already been made.

The meal that's just for us is an opportunity to enjoy adult flavors that kids don't necessarily like. It's a chance to indulge in a bold cocktail, like a Negroni (page 265) or Caipirinha (page 264). The Pecorino and Honey Dip (page 26) is a wonderful, mood-setting appetizer for date night, as are the Fried Squash Blossoms (page 36). We might indulge in a Risotto with Squab and Mushrooms (page 102) or the intensely flavored Spaghetti Puttanesca (page 62). Dessert adds something rich and decadent, so we might make a fruit tart or Panna Cotta (page 240) well in advance and let it sit in the refrigerator. It's a chance for us to make the most of our more elegant menu favorites. Then, when that blissful silence is all that's detectable from the children's rooms, the real show begins. We'll bring out a nice, rarely used tablecloth, the good dishware, and cloth napkins. One of us will light the candles and turn on the playlist, at an appropriately soft volume. Then we get dressed. That's right: we *eagerly* shed our everyday clothes and treat the upcoming hours as if we had a reservation at a fancy restaurant. We turn home into the most romantic place in town.

Date night has taken all kinds of turns with us. It's been fast and frisky, slow and luxurious, and sometimes the day has just been too exhausting to do much but eat quickly and fall asleep. But at heart it's not about the tablecloth, or the flowers, or the food. It's about the time and energy we put into making a moment for us to be together.

desserts

DOLCI

near a *gelateria*. But our pleasure in sweets isn't predicated on intensely filling, elaborate concoctions. Although you can find complicated cakes and desserts in Italy, you're just as likely to find a wonderful meal ending with something as simple as fruit, a pastry, a bite of chocolate, or a scoop of gelato with a cookie. The perfect punctuation mark to a beautiful sentence is what a sweet bite should evoke.

D: I think of dessert as an indulgence, but one that should bring about the same warm, homey feelings that your entree hopefully aroused. When you have children, they're likely to think of dessert as the main course.

G: But for me, if we've just had ribs, my dessert might be one more rib!

D: Which just goes to show that we approach desserts as a complement to a menu, but something that should also be able to stand on its own. In our diet-conscious world, how often at restaurants do you hear your tablemates saying, "I couldn't possibly eat anything else," and then as soon as someone orders a sorbet, and someone else thinks they'll try the tiramisu, everyone's got room for a bite? That's why our desserts aren't the kind that weigh you down: they bring you in for a soft, happy, delicious landing.

G: It's become a sort of perceived wisdom that Italians are not wild and crazy dessert eaters, but I want to make something clear: We definitely enjoy our sweets. Talk to my ten-year-old self when he was wolfing down a bag of Cenci di Carnevale (page 236), or my dad when he has a syrupy Macedonia (page 257) in front of him, or any Italian on a blazing summer day when

G: These recipes aren't solely about the sweet end to an evening. There are cookies and tarts that could bring a smile to any afternoon tea or coffee, and a few items that—trust me on this— you'll want for breakfast. This chapter is about the many ways you can add a hint of sweetness to the day, and the recipes certainly don't require a master *pasticcere* (pastry chef).

SEMOLINA ROSEMARY PIGNOLI COOKIES

BISCOTTI PINOLI E ROSMARINO

G: *When we bake these, that aroma of pine nuts, rosemary, and butter brings me back to Christmases with Nonna Lola and the baskets of goodies she'd bring to the house. The rosemary gives these cookies that extra Tuscan touch, as if they sprang from a garden, rather than an oven.*

½ cup pine nuts (pignoli)

2 sticks (½ pound) butter, at room temperature

1 cup sugar

1 large egg

1¾ cups all-purpose flour

½ cup fine semolina flour

¼ teaspoon salt

2 teaspoons fresh rosemary

1 teaspoon grated orange zest

In a small skillet, lightly toast the pine nuts over high heat for 3 to 4 minutes. Remove from the heat and transfer to a bowl to cool.

In a stand mixer fitted with the paddle attachment, combine the butter and sugar and beat until light and fluffy. Add the egg and mix until well combined.

In a medium bowl, combine the all-purpose flour, semolina flour, salt, rosemary, and orange zest. With the mixer on low speed, slowly add the flour mixture to the butter mixture, until the dough forms and starts detaching from the sides of the bowl. Add the toasted pine nuts and stir to combine.

Divide the dough into 2 equal pieces. Roll each piece into a log about 10 inches long and 2 inches in diameter. Wrap them in plastic and refrigerate for at least 1 hour or overnight.

Preheat the oven to 350°F. Line two 9 × 13-inch baking sheets with parchment paper.

Slice a cookie dough log crosswise into ¼-inch-thick rounds. Place the rounds on the lined sheets, leaving about 1 inch of space between cookies. (If they need to be reshaped or look too thick, you can gently pat them down to the desired shape and size.)

Bake for 12 minutes, rotating the pans front to back halfway through. The cookies should be deep golden brown on the bottom and look dry on top. Transfer the cookies to wire racks to cool. Repeat with the second dough log.

CHESTNUT FLOUR CAKE

CASTAGNACCIO

This seasonal fall cake is deeply rooted in Tuscan tradition—a savory, nutty celebration of chestnuts with only a delicate sweetness because of the raisins. It resembles a flatbread, because it doesn't use yeast and therefore won't rise. But that has made it a perennial favorite of hunters, since it can be sliced and stored in a pouch without breaking. It's also peasant in origin, due to the use of inexpensive chestnut flour. After a meat-heavy meal, and accompanied by a glass of wine, it has an earthy dignity, one that's satisfied Tuscans for generations.

4 tablespoons extra virgin olive oil

1 pound sweet chestnut flour

2 tablespoons sugar

Pinch of salt

Grated zest of ½ orange

2 ounces raisins, soaked in water for 20 minutes and drained

1 tablespoon fresh rosemary leaves, whole

1 ounce chopped walnuts

1 ounce pine nuts (pignoli)

Preheat the oven to 375°F. Lightly grease an 11-inch pie plate (one with 2-inch-high sides) with 1 tablespoon of the olive oil.

Sift the chestnut flour into a large bowl. Mix in the sugar, salt, and orange zest. Gently stir in 2 cups water.

Using a hand mixer, beat the mixture well, making sure to eliminate any lumps. Add 2 tablespoons of the olive oil and half the raisins, and mix again.

Pour the mixture into the pie plate; it should be no more than ⅓ inch thick. Sprinkle the cake with the rosemary, walnuts, pine nuts, and remaining raisins. Drizzle the remaining 1 tablespoon olive oil on top. Bake for 40 minutes, or until the top is chestnut brown and begins to crack, and wrinkle-like lines begin to form.

Remove from the oven, slice, and serve.

ALMOND COOKIES

BISCOTTI DI PRATO

———————————— MAKES 50 ————————————

D: *These delicious cookies—made with toasted almonds and baked to a satisfying crunch—are a traditional Italian treat and Tuscan through and through. And they are addictive. We fill up a jar, and before we know it, it's empty.*

G: *Nowadays you can find biscotti in all variety of flavors, but in Tuscany, it's almonds all the way. The common way to enjoy biscotti is to dip them in the fortified, sweet dessert wine known as Vin Santo. But you could also dunk them in coffee or tea. They're perfect after a meal, or to help pass a lazy afternoon.*

6 ounces unsalted raw skin-on almonds

2⅔ cups all-purpose unbleached flour

1 (16-gram) envelope Lievito Pane degli Angeli (Italian leavening with vanilla, see note)

Pinch of salt

Grated zest of 1 orange

1¼ cups sugar

3 large eggs

3 large egg yolks

1 tablespoon unsalted butter, melted, plus more for greasing the baking sheet

Vin Santo (or coffee or tea), for serving

Preheat the oven to 375°F.

On a baking sheet, place the almonds and toast them in the oven for about 10 minutes. Transfer to a wide ceramic platter to cool. (Do not leave them on the baking sheet or they will burn.)

In a small bowl, whisk together the flour, leavening, salt, and orange zest.

In a large bowl, mix together the sugar, 2 of the whole eggs, and all of the egg yolks, making sure to work out the lumps. Stir in the melted butter.

Add the flour mixture to the bowl with the egg mixture and mix well. When the dough is smooth, mix in the toasted almonds.

Grease a baking sheet with butter. Using your hands, divide the dough in half and form 2 loaves of equal length, approximately 2 inches thick.

In a small bowl, whisk the remaining egg. Brush the beaten egg over the loaves.

Bake for 20 minutes, or until the tops have a golden brown color.

Remove from the oven and cut the loaves crosswise into ½-inch slices. Return the cookies to the oven, separated and standing up, and bake an additional 5 minutes until dry. Remove from the oven and let cool on a wire rack for 5 minutes, or until completely cooled.

For ideal crunchiness, let the cookies rest uncovered overnight. The next day, toast them in a 350°F oven for 10 minutes, then let cool. Serve with the dunking beverage of your choice.

IMPORTANTE! Lievito Pane degli Angeli means "the yeast bread of angels." It's a leavening agent infused with vanilla, essentially the Italian version of baking powder, and a staple in every Italian baker's home. Any good Italian deli should carry it, and it's also widely available via the Internet. (Bertolini Lievito is another Italian brand of vanilla-infused leavening, and works just as well.)

CARNIVAL FRITTERS

CENCI DI CARNEVALE

G: *As much as certain vegetables mark seasonal parts of the Italian food calendar, so do the sweet snacks that herald the festive Carnival season, which began in Venice but is celebrated throughout Italy. Because it's specifically tied to the period before Lent, it's the time to indulge! In Tuscany, the big favorites are Rice Fritters (opposite) and these fried pastry strips, called* cenci, *which translates roughly as "rags." They're fluffy, crumbly, and crunchy, and when you buy them from bakeries in Italy, they come in a brown bag stained with oil. Believe me, for a kid craving deep-fried dough, that's a good sign!*

2 cups all-purpose flour, plus more for dusting

¼ cup granulated sugar

3 tablespoons unsalted butter, melted, at room temperature

2 large eggs

1 shot (1½ ounces) Vin Santo (or rum or brandy)

Grated zest of 1 orange

4 cups safflower, vegetable, or canola oil, for deep-frying

Confectioners' sugar, for dusting

In a stand mixer fitted with the dough hook, combine the flour, granulated sugar, melted butter, eggs, Vin Santo, and orange zest. Mix for 5 to 7 minutes, until the dough begins detaching from the sides of the bowl.

Remove the dough from the bowl, seal it in plastic wrap, and refrigerate for 30 minutes.

On a work surface lightly dusted with flour, roll the dough until it's as thin as fresh pasta. (A pasta machine can also be used for this part.) Using a pastry wheel or pizza cutter, slice the dough into 5-inch-long, 1-inch-wide strips.

In a high-sided skillet, add the oil to a level of 2 inches. Heat the oil over high heat until a deep-fry thermometer reads 360°F. Fry the strips of dough (the *cenci*) in batches, flipping occasionally, for 4 to 5 minutes per batch, until they curl slightly and acquire a golden brown color.

Transfer the *cenci* to a platter lined with paper towels to absorb the excess oil. Dust with the confectioners' sugar and serve with a glass of Vin Santo.

CARNIVAL RICE FRITTERS

FRITTELLE DI SAN GIUSEPPE

• SERVES 8 •

G: *Here are Carnival goodies, part two! These fritters—made with rice, Vin Santo-soaked raisins, and a dusting of sugar—named after St. Joseph are heavenly. Fun to make, they're even more fun to eat, especially with a shot of Vin Santo, rum, or brandy.*

¼ cup raisins

2 shots (3 ounces) Vin Santo (or brandy or rum)

2 cups whole milk

4 tablespoons sugar

2 tablespoons unsalted butter

2 pinches of salt

1 cup long-grain white rice

2 tablespoons all-purpose flour

2 large egg yolks

1 teaspoon grated lemon zest

4 cups safflower, canola, or vegetable oil, for deep-frying

In a small bowl, combine the raisins, 1 shot of the Vin Santo, and enough water so the raisins are just covered. Let sit for 30 minutes so the raisins can soften.

In a 2-quart pot, combine 1 cup water, the milk, 2 tablespoons of the sugar, the butter, and salt, and bring to a boil. Add the rice, reduce the heat to medium-low, and cook for about 20 minutes, or until all the liquid has been absorbed. Remove from the heat and transfer the rice to a large bowl to let cool. Stir the rice as it cools to keep the grains from sticking to each other.

Drain the raisins.

In the large bowl with the cooked rice, add the flour, egg yolks, lemon zest, the remaining shot of Vin Santo, and the drained raisins. Mix well, cover with plastic wrap, and refrigerate for at least 1 hour or overnight.

In a high-sided skillet, add the oil to a level of 2 inches. Heat over high heat until a deep-fry thermometer reads 360°F. Using a tablespoon or a small ice cream scoop, add small balls of the rice mixture to the hot oil. Move the *frittelle* around to ensure even frying, about 4 to 5 minutes per batch, and when they are a nice golden brown, transfer them to a plate lined with paper towels to absorb the excess oil.

Place the remaining 2 tablespoons sugar in a cereal bowl. When the *frittelle* have slightly cooled, use your hands to roll them in the sugar until they are lightly dusted.

FLORENTINE ORANGE CAKE

SCHIACCIATA ALLA FIORENTINA

———— • SERVES 12 • ————

D: *This traditional Tuscan cake is also celebrated at Carnival. The sweet-and-sugary indulgences of Carnival are in some measure a delicious way to mark the end of winter's desserts before arriving at the fruits and vegetables of spring. The orangey pleasures in* the schiacciata *are a light teaser for the harvested pleasures to come. Where Gabriele's from, the cake always comes with a confectioners' sugar stencil of a Florentine lily, too.*

Unsalted butter, for greasing the pan

3 large eggs

1 cup granulated sugar

¼ cup vegetable oil

½ cup whole milk, warmed

1½ cups all-purpose flour

1 (16-gram) envelope Lievito Pane degli Angeli (see note, page 235) or 1½ tablespoons baking powder

Grated zest and juice of 1 orange

Confectioners' sugar, for topping

Preheat the oven to 350°F. Grease a 13 × 9-inch baking pan with butter.

In a large bowl, combine the eggs, granulated sugar, oil, milk, flour, Italian leavening (or baking powder), orange zest and orange juice. Using a hand mixer, beat the mixture for 3 to 4 minutes, until the texture is creamy and mildly thick.

Spread the batter in the baking pan, and bake for about 30 minutes, until a toothpick inserted into the center comes out dry and the cake has risen threefold.

Remove from the oven and let cool for 30 minutes. Then flip the cake out of the baking pan onto a cutting board. Slice and serve sprinkled with confectioners' sugar.

IMPORTANTE! If you're looking for a fun edible craft project, you can stencil a design or lettering using the confectioners' sugar.

PANNA COTTA

D: *A simple, time-honored Italian custard, the* panna cotta—*which means "cooked cream"—doesn't take long to make, and the luxurious pleasure it yields can be considerable. What I love about this recipe is that even though it involves heavy cream, the proportion of gelatin to dairy—and the use of whole milk—produces a lighter taste. Serve it with chocolate sauce (the way I like it) or fresh berries (my husband's preferred choice)!*

1 cup whole milk

1 cup heavy cream

¾ cup confectioners' sugar

1 vanilla bean, split lengthwise (not going all the way through)

1¼ teaspoons unflavored powdered gelatin

In a medium saucepan, combine the milk, cream, and confectioners' sugar. Scrape the vanilla seeds into the pan and add the vanilla pod. Heat over medium heat until it comes to a near-boil. Reduce the heat to low.

In a small bowl, sprinkle 3 tablespoons water over the gelatin and mix well to soften the gelatin. Add to the hot cream in the skillet and stir well for 1 minute to dissolve the gelatin.

Remove from the heat and strain through a fine-mesh strainer into a medium bowl. Using a ladle, divide the cream among six 4-ounce metal molds. Let them rest for 15 minutes, then refrigerate for at least 3 hours to set.

In a bowl just large enough to fit the molds in, prepare an ice bath. When ready to serve, dip the metal molds in the ice bath, one by one, for 15 seconds each. (Don't let the water touch the panna cotta.) Flip each panna cotta onto a small dessert plate and serve.

IMPORTANTE! If the panna cotta doesn't dislodge easily, you can use a small paring knife to separate the dessert from the metal sides.

RICOTTA PANCAKES

PANCAKES DI RICOTTA

• SERVES 4 •

D: *This dish began as a surprise birthday present from my husband, because he knows how much I love pancakes. He enlisted our daughters one birthday morning—breaking eggs, fluffing the whites—and these Tuscan-influenced gems were the result. The lemon zest adds a kick, and they're delicately creamy because of the ricotta. Plus, they're lighter tasting than your typical buttermilk slabs. (Though I like a stack of those, too!)*

4 large eggs, separated

1 ½ cups whole milk ricotta cheese

1 tablespoon sugar

Grated zest of ½ lemon

Pinch of kosher salt

½ cup all-purpose flour

Unsalted butter, for greasing the griddle

Maple syrup, for serving

Heat a nonstick griddle over medium-high heat. Preheat the oven to 200°F.

In a large bowl, mix together the egg yolks, ricotta, sugar, lemon zest, salt, and flour until thoroughly combined.

In a separate bowl, beat the egg whites until stiff peaks form. Fold the whites into the ricotta in one-third amounts, mixing gently to maintain as much volume as possible.

Grease the hot griddle with butter. For each pancake, ladle ½ cup pancake batter onto the griddle and cook for 2 minutes per side, until golden and crisp on the edges. Keep the pancakes warm in the oven. Serve the pancakes with maple syrup.

PLUM JAM

MARMELLATA DI PRUGNE

MAKES 8–10 POUNDS

G: *Making jam is a true family undertaking at our home in Tuscany. Everyone pitches in to pick the fruit, then we help prep for my mother, who cooks down the fruit for hours. It's a tradition as important to us as making olive oil or tomato sauce. This recipe, based on a 2:1 ratio of fruit to sugar, yields a more tart-tasting than sweet jam. Remember to keep tasting your jam as you cook the fruit, because the acidity level depends on the quality of the fruit you're using. You can always adjust the flavor with more or less sugar. The finished jam tastes great on bread or over ice cream. Also, try this recipe with apricots—the results are equally delicious!*

10 pounds plums, washed, halved, and pitted

1 (5-pound) bag sugar (about 11 cups)

In a large stockpot, cook the plums over medium heat until boiling.

Add the sugar, reduce the heat to medium-low, and stir well to avoid burning the fruit on the bottom of the pot. Cook for about 3 hours, or until the desired thickness, stirring every 10 to 15 minutes. Remove from the heat and let cool, stirring every 10 minutes, for about 1 hour. Store in the refrigerator.

IMPORTANTE! Preserving jam in jars is easy, and it can last for up to 1 year when stored properly. Using a funnel with a wide hole, transfer the cooked fruit to 8-ounce or 12-ounce sterilized glass jars, leaving room to add 2 tablespoons of grappa, aquavit, or brandy on top. (Be sure that you've properly sterilized your materials before canning—there are a number of easy-to-follow guidelines on the Web for how to do so.) Cover the jars with plastic wrap and tightly close with the cap. Store in a cool, dark place—such as a basement or cellar. When ready to eat, remove the cap and plastic wrap, stir the 2-tablespoon layer of liquor into the jam, and serve. Refrigerate after opening, after which the jam will keep for 1 month.

FIG JAM TART

CROSTATA DI FICHI

D: *Already one of my favorite jams when it comes to all things spreadable, fig jam nestled in a tart takes that deliciousness to the next level. Gabriele and I have been known to get cravings for this in the middle of the night when we know there's still some left in the house, so let that be a warning when you make it! However, if you can wait until the sun rises, it's a perfectly fruity, not-too-sweet, rustic slice to go with your morning coffee, too.*

2½ cups all-purpose flour, plus more for rolling

½ cup sugar

Pinch of salt

Grated zest of 1 orange

1 vanilla bean, split lengthwise (not going all the way through)

2 sticks (½ pound) unsalted butter, cut into ½-inch pieces and chilled, plus more for greasing the pan

3 large egg yolks

¼ cup plus 3 tablespoons grappa or rum

1½ cups fig jam

In a stand mixer fitted with the paddle attachment, combine the flour, sugar, salt, and orange zest and mix for about 30 seconds. Scrape in the vanilla seeds and add the chilled butter. Mix at medium speed for 3 to 5 minutes, or until the mixture looks like coarse crumbs.

In a small bowl, beat the egg yolks with ¼ cup of the grappa, then add it to the dough mixture and mix for 30 seconds to 1 minute, until the dough begins to detach from the sides of the bowl. Transfer the dough to a work surface and shape it into a disc. Cover it with plastic wrap and refrigerate it for at least 1 hour.

Preheat the oven to 400°F. Grease an 11-inch tart pan with a removable bottom with butter.

In a small bowl, stir together the fig jam and the remaining 3 tablespoons grappa, mixing well.

On a floured surface, roll the dough to a round about ⅛ inch thick and gently place it in the tart pan. Press the dough lightly against the sides. Using your fingers, press the dough against the rim of the pan to cut off the excess dough. Using a fork, poke the dough all the way through to the pan surface several times. (This will allow the oven's hot air to come through.) Using a spoon, spread the jam on top of the dough.

Bake the tart for 25 minutes, until golden brown. Remove from the oven, let cool, and serve.

LEMON BRÛLÉ TART

CROSTATA DI LIMONE BRÛLÉ

· SERVES 6–8 ·

G: *What I love about a tart is what I love about Tuscan cooking in general—it becomes an elegantly simple vehicle for whatever flavor I want to showcase. In this case, that's the sensual, citrusy joy of a lemon brûlé. Plus, I must admit, wielding the torch for the final caramelization on top is a lot of fun, like I'm welding dessert!*

DOUGH

2½ cups all-purpose flour

½ cup granulated sugar

Pinch of salt

Grated zest of 1 lemon

1 vanilla bean, split lengthwise (not going all the way through)

2 sticks (½ pound) unsalted butter, cut into ½-inch pieces and chilled, plus more for greasing the pan

1 large egg, separated

2 large egg yolks

1 shot (1½ ounces) grappa or rum

FILLING

1 cup granulated sugar

1 cup heavy cream

5 large egg yolks

2 large eggs

Grated zest and juice of 2 lemons

2 tablespoons confectioners' sugar

To make the dough: In a stand mixer fitted with the dough hook, combine the flour, granulated sugar, salt, and lemon zest, and mix for 30 seconds. Scrape in the vanilla seeds and add the butter. Mix on medium speed for 3 to 5 minutes, until the mixture looks like coarse crumbs.

In a small bowl, mix together the 3 egg yolks and the grappa. Add it to the dough mixture while the machine is running and mix on medium speed for 30 seconds to 1 minute, until the dough detaches from the sides of the bowl. Transfer the dough to a work surface and shape it into a disc. Cover it with plastic wrap and refrigerate for at least 1 hour.

Meanwhile, **to make the filling:** In a large bowl, whisk together the granulated sugar, cream, egg yolks, and whole eggs. Whisk in the lemon zest and juice.

Preheat the oven to 375°F. Butter an 11-inch tart pan with a removable bottom.

On a floured surface, roll the dough to a round about ⅛ inch thick and gently place it in the tart pan. Press the dough lightly against the sides. Using your fingers, press the dough against the rim of the pan to cut off the excess dough. Using a fork, poke the dough all the way through to the pan surface several times. (This will allow the oven's hot air to come through.) Brush the dough with a thin layer of the egg white.

Place a baking sheet on the rack below the tart to protect the oven from spillage. Bake for 25 to 30 minutes, or until the edges of the dough look golden and crisp. Remove the tart shell from the oven and reduce the oven temperature to 300°F.

Place the tart on a baking sheet and pour the filling into the warm shell. Tap gently on the counter to release any excess air bubbles in the filling. Return the tart to the oven and bake for 40 minutes, or until the filling appears firm but with a slight jiggle in the center.

Remove from the oven and let cool for about 30 minutes. Remove the tart from the pan sides and sprinkle evenly with the confectioners' sugar. Using a crème brûlée torch, caramelize the sugar on top. Serve immediately.

COFFEE GRANITA

GRANITA AL CAFFÈ

The flavored ice treat known as granita *is immensely popular in Italy's hot months. The younger set likes to cool off with fruity granitas, and coffee or liquor is great for a more sophisticated flavor. For our coffee version, rather than just pouring espresso over freshly scraped ice, we use a freezing and refreezing technique that takes a little more time, but results in a fantastic, fluffy ice-and-coffee taste.*

2 cups freshly brewed espresso

2 tablespoons sugar

¼ cup heavy cream

1 vanilla bean, split lengthwise (not going all the way through)

In a medium bowl, stir together the hot espresso and sugar until the sugar dissolves. Let cool for 20 minutes, then pour into a wide plastic container, cover with a lid, and freeze for 1 hour.

Remove from the freezer. Using a fork, break up the ice, stir it, cover with the lid, then return it to the freezer. Repeat this process every 30 minutes for 3 hours, until the coffee ice is translucent and like crystals.

Place the cream in a medium bowl and scrape in the vanilla seeds. Mix with a hand mixer on high speed for 4 to 5 minutes, until soft peaks form.

Serve the coffee ice in tall thin glasses, each topped with a tablespoon of whipped cream. The coffee *granita* will stay good in the freezer for a couple of days.

TIRAMISÙ

D: *I love what* tiramisù *means—"pick me up." But it wasn't until I had it in Tuscany that I came to appreciate it. All the* tiramisu *I'd had before were overlayered, containing too much cream, and intensely sweetened. More like, "pick me up then watch me crash."*

G: *That's because American* tiramisu *often uses heavy cream and sugar. Real mascarpone cream is actually an unsweetened cream cheese, buttery but not sweet. A proper* tiramisu *achieves the right balance of coffee, cookie, chocolate, and cream.*

D: *It's like getting a complex dessert without cooking or baking.*

5 large fresh organic eggs, separated

½ cup sugar

1 pound mascarpone

Pinch of salt

2 shots (3 ounces) rum or Italian Marsala (optional)

3 cups brewed coffee sweetened with 2 tablespoons sugar, cooled

14 ounces savoiardi cookies (Italian ladyfingers)

2 tablespoons unsweetened cocoa powder

¼ cup shaved dark chocolate, for garnish (optional)

In a medium bowl, beat together the egg yolks and ¼ cup of the sugar until light and creamy.

In a separate medium bowl, work the mascarpone with a wooden spoon until all lumps are eliminated. Add the egg yolk mixture and mix well.

In a third medium bowl, combine the egg whites, salt, and remaining ¼ cup of sugar, and beat until they reach a slightly firm but fluffy consistency. Gently fold the egg white mixture into the mascarpone mixture, one ladle at a time, stirring from the bottom up to help maintain as much volume as possible, until the egg whites are fully incorporated. Stir in the rum (if using).

Place the coffee in a fourth medium bowl. Dip each cookie into the coffee (don't soak the them; you want them to retain their firmness) and then arrange in a 7 × 11-inch glass baking dish until the bottom is covered. Over the first layer of cookies, spread half the mascarpone cream, and dust with 1 tablespoon cocoa powder. Repeat with another layer of cookies, mascarpone cream, and cocoa powder.

Cover the dish with plastic wrap and refrigerate for 3 hours. Garnish the top with the shaved chocolate and serve chilled.

OLIVE OIL GELATO
with cherry compote

GELATO OLIO DI OLIVA CON COMPOTE CILIEGIA

MAKES 1½ QUARTS

G: *Deborah and I developed this as a tribute of sorts to my Nonna, who has spent so much of her life making food and passing down recipes. So we wanted to show her how well we could interpret her advice and guidance. She never made ice cream, but by infusing a vanilla gelato with olive oil from our property, it was a way of giving her thanks. There's a piece of our land in everything we do.*

D: *It's almost like a memory of olive oil is inside, since it's not about overwhelming the gelato, but finding that back flavor, that hint of sweet bitterness you get from high-end olive oil. With the added tartness of cherries on top, it's a lush, beautiful merging of flavors.*

2¾ cups whole milk

1¼ cups heavy cream

1 vanilla bean, split lengthwise (not going all the way through)

7 large egg yolks

1 cup sugar

Pinch of salt

¾ cup extra virgin olive oil

Cherry Compote (recipe follows)

In a heavy-bottomed saucepan, combine the milk and heavy cream. Scrape in the vanilla seeds and add the vanilla pod. Bring to a very low simmer over medium heat, stirring often.

Meanwhile, in a large bowl, whisk together the egg yolks, sugar, and salt until light and fluffy, about 3 minutes. Whisk in the olive oil and beat vigorously for 1 minute, until completely emulsified.

Slowly ladle about 1 cup of the hot milk mixture into the egg yolk mixture, whisking constantly to prevent the eggs from scrambling. Add the warmed egg mixture to the saucepan with the remaining milk and stir for 5 to 6 minutes, until it thickens slightly and coats the back of a spoon.

Strain the custard through a fine-mesh strainer into a large 8-cup measuring vessel. Let cool, then cover with plastic wrap, and refrigerate for about 3 hours, or until well chilled. (This can also be refrigerated overnight.)

Using an ice cream maker, freeze the custard according to the manufacturer's directions, at least 30 minutes, until it achieves a soft-serve consistency. Transfer to the freezer, and freeze for 1 hour, or until firm. The texture of gelato should be creamy, so be careful not to freeze it for too long.

Serve in bowls topped with warm Cherry Compote.

CHERRY COMPOTE
COMPOTE CILIEGIA
MAKES 2–3 CUPS

1 quart cherries, pitted

1 tablespoon sugar, or more to taste

Grated zest of 1 lemon

2 to 3 tablespoons dark rum, to taste

In a 2-quart saucepan, combine ½ cup water, the cherries, sugar, and lemon zest and bring to a low simmer over medium heat, stirring so the sugar dissolves completely. Cook for 7 to 10 minutes, until the cherries just begin to break up. (Depending on the ripeness of your cherries, this may take longer.)

Remove from the heat and stir in the rum. Return it to the heat, ignite the compote safely with a long-handled lighter like a long fireplace match, and cook for 30 seconds to 1 minute to reduce the alcohol content. Blow on the flame to extinguish it.

Serve warm over the Olive Oil Gelato (opposite).

MASCARPONE AND AMARETTI CUPS

TAZZINE DI MASCARPONE E AMARETTI

—·— SERVES 6 —·—

D: *We developed this recipe for a grown-ups' party as a simplified twist on Tiramisù (page 248). It's all the pleasure of cookies and mascarpone cream without the added buzz of espresso. The single dose of sweet dairy thickness with the almondy crunch of the amaretti cookies is irresistible. Another reason it's a great party dessert? You can make it in advance and keep it refrigerated for 1 day.*

3 large eggs, separated

4 tablespoons sugar

8 ounces mascarpone

Pinch of salt

1½ cups roughly crumbled amaretti cookies

½ shot (¾ ounce) brandy

Dash of unsweetened cocoa powder, plus more for garnish

Shaved dark chocolate, for garnish

Fresh seasonal berries, for garnish

Fresh mint sprigs, for garnish

In a medium bowl, beat the egg yolks and 2 tablespoons of the sugar until the texture is creamy.

In a separate medium bowl, work the mascarpone with a wooden spoon until all the lumps are eliminated. Add the mascarpone to the egg yolk mixture and mix well.

In a third medium bowl, beat the the egg whites, salt, and remaining 2 tablespoons of sugar until the whites are somewhat firm and form stiff peaks. Fold the egg white mixture into the mascarpone mixture, one ladle at a time, spooning from the bottom to the top, until fully incorporated. The resulting cream should be rich, yet soft and fluffy.

In a fourth medium bowl, combine the crumbled cookies and brandy. Stir until just softened but not soggy, then stir in the cocoa powder. Divide the cookie mixture among 6 glasses.

Fill a piping bag with the mascarpone cream and pipe the cream into each glass. Top with a sprinkle of cocoa powder and shaved dark chocolate. Garnish with berries and a sprig of mint.

IMPORTANTE! For a rustic feel, serve this in cappuccino cups. For a fancier presentation, it looks great in martini glasses.

ROASTED PEACHES
with amaretti filling

PESCHE GRIGLIATE CON RIPIENO DI AMARETTI

───────────────────────────── SERVES 6 ─────────────────────────────

This summery delectable is great on barbecue days. The caramelized outer layer of sugar from grilling the peaches, plus the cookies and liqueur, with that grace note of chocolate, makes for a wonderful flavor combination.

6 peaches, halved and pitted

¾ cup crumbled amaretti cookies

1 tablespoon unsweetened cocoa powder

¼ cup amaretto liqueur

Preheat a grill to medium-high heat, or prepare a charcoal grill until the coals are bright red.

Place the peaches cut-side down on the grill and grill for 3 minutes, until golden and slightly charred. Turn them over and cook for another 3 minutes, until softened. Remove from the grill and let cool.

In a medium bowl, combine the cookie crumbs, cocoa powder, and amaretto and toss well. Shape the cookie crumbles into 12 balls. Place 1 ball in the center of each half peach. Serve warm.

LEMON SORBET

———————————— MAKES 1 QUART ————————————

We get a lot of use out of our ice cream machine every summer. If you have one too, try our lemon sorbet, which uses our homemade Limoncello (page 262). One of life's great refreshers, sorbet is not only a great meal-ending palate cleanser, but can also be a wonderful way to introduce children to a sweet, cold fruit-flavored treat that isn't ice cream. On a hot day, the silky texture and sharp lemony taste of this sorbet is simply blissful.

1 cup sugar

2 teaspoons grated lemon zest

1 cup lemon juice (from about 6 lemons)

3 tablespoons Limoncello (page 262) or store-bought

In a medium saucepan, combine 1 cup water, the sugar, and lemon zest and stir over medium heat until the sugar has dissolved. Add 1½ cups cold water, the lemon juice, and the Limoncello. Transfer to a plastic container, cover with a lid, and refrigerate until chilled, about 2 hours.

Using an ice cream maker, freeze the cold lemon mixture according to the manufacturer's directions, until the sorbet has a soft-serve consistency. Transfer to a plastic lidded container and freeze until firm, about 3 hours.

Serve in small bowls or parfait cups.

FRUIT SALAD

MACEDONIA

D: *One way to get kids to eat fruit is to just call fruit a dessert!*

G: *No kidding. My brother and I never perceived of a* macedonia *as fruit. It always felt like a treat. But there's method behind it: if you add a touch of sugar and allow it to pull juices out of the fruit while it sits in the fridge, the nectar it creates at the bottom is just fantastic.*

D: *It's a great way to use up whatever fruit is still lying around, that half apple, or slightly overripe banana. They add interesting textures along with the berries. So think of the ingredients below as a guideline, and come up with your own fruit combos!*

1 pound strawberries, quartered

1 pint blueberries

1 pint blackberries

1 pint raspberries

Juice of 3 oranges

Juice of 1 lemon

2 tablespoons sugar (optional)

Handful of fresh mint leaves, chopped

In a large bowl, combine the strawberries, blueberries, blackberries, raspberries, orange juice, lemon juice, sugar (if using), and mint. Cover with plastic wrap and refrigerate for 3 hours.

Serve in small bowls.

drinks

BEVANDE

INDEX

D: Highly trained mixologists may be all the rage in today's trendy bars and restaurants, but we think it's important to know that you don't need a fully stocked bar or a degree in aroma extraction and ice management to be able to enjoy the occasional refreshing mixed beverage. Having a few essential liquors and ingredients on hand though, can go a long way toward making that special something to entertain dinner guests, or to kick off a sexy, romantic evening or enjoy a languid weekend afternoon.

G: That's why we kept this section to a handful of what we consider indispensable pleasure-stirrers, primarily Italian or South American in origin. We're big fans of citrusy concoctions with some muddled fruit element, and maybe a touch of sweetness. If we're making one of these drinks, however, we're not likely to move to a different alcohol, such as red wine. If we have a Caipirinha (page 264) before dinner because we think its flavors go so well with the menu, we'll maybe follow it up with one more during the meal. We're not inclined to mix.

D: Above all, we believe a cocktail should be happy-making, whether it comes before or after the food. So we hope that with these delicious creations you get that tinge of elegant, grown-up fun we all need sometimes.

LIMONCELLO

D: *I'll never forget sipping on homemade limoncello for the first time. It was before I met Gabriele, on a trip to the south of Italy. What a treat: icy, fresh-tasting, and the ideal lemony palate cleanser after a summer meal.*

G: *Homemade is the way to go, and it's really the only way I knew, because my aunt Laura made it every summer. When we were in our teens, Nonna would treat my brother and me to a small shot of it after private dinners with her in summertime. It was very conspiratorial, since she didn't want any other adults to know, but man, was it fantastic.*

D: *So get ready, because this bottle of liqueur will fly out of your freezer during the hot months. But it requires some patience: two weeks for the lemon peels to infuse, and a month for the whole mixture to achieve liquid-gold status.*

G: *Adjust the sugar levels to your liking, too. We prefer limoncello on the less-sweet side (which this recipe reflects), but you may enjoy a sweeter swallow.*

2 (750 ml) bottles grain alcohol   **4½ cups sugar**

Zest of 14 lemons

In a 5-quart, round-mouthed glass jar, combine the alcohol and lemon zest. Tightly seal the jar and store it in darkness—preferably a cellar or basement—for 2 weeks.

When ready to make the limoncello, strain the alcohol into a large pot or bowl, discard the lemon zest, then return the infused alcohol to the large jar.

In a 4-quart pot, combine 1½ liters water and the sugar. Bring to a soft boil, stirring occasionally until the sugar is dissolved. Set aside for at least 1 hour to cool.

Add the sugar water to the jar with the infused alcohol and seal tightly. If you notice sugar deposits at the bottom of the jar, shake it gently. Store in darkness again, for 1 month.

Transfer to 500 ml (or smaller) bottles and serve well chilled in shot glasses. Limoncello is best kept in the freezer until it's ready to serve.

IMPORTANTE! Bottled homemade limoncello makes a wonderful gift for friends, as we've detected from the countless smiling faces over the years!

LIMONCELLO SPRITZER

Once you've made Limoncello (opposite), enjoy the cocktail version! The spritzer element comes from Prosecco, the dry, young, Italian sparkling wine with often delicate fruit notes that's extremely popular as an aperitif. This garden-party spritzer is a fun, bubbly, berry-tinged way to get that lemony buzz.

1 pint raspberries, plus more for garnish   **1 (750 ml) bottle Prosecco, chilled**

½ cup Limoncello (opposite), chilled

In a food processor, purée the raspberries until smooth. Strain the raspberry purée through a fine-mesh strainer into a pitcher.

Add the limoncello and Prosecco and stir. Garnish with extra raspberries and serve immediately in 6 ice-filled glasses.

CAIPIRINHA

⊷ SERVES 1 ⊷

D: *Gabriele became familiar with this Brazilian cocktail after spending time in that country, and when he introduced it to me, I fell in love with it. Since that introduction happened to be in a bar off the Piazza Santo Spirito in Florence, on the hot summer evening that we first met, it's a drink I hold near and dear to my heart. Sexy, light, and minty, the caipirinha is made with a fermented sugar cane liquor called* cachaça, *which you should be able to find at most liquor stores.*

½ **lime, sliced into small chunks**

1 teaspoon raw sugar

2 ounces cachaça

In a cocktail shaker, muddle the lime and sugar together.

Fill a highball glass with crushed ice and add the cachaça. Pour the cachaça and ice into the cocktail shaker and shake. Transfer the cachaça mixture back into the highball glass and serve with a straw.

NEGRONI

(pictured on page 258)

─── • SERVES 1 • ───

D: *Strong, vivacious, and emboldening, the Negroni is a swanky bar classic. We've always believed that when we see someone at a party drinking a Negroni that he or she has character, and is probably worth getting to know. And it's a drink you can see from across the room: a brilliant dark red, with that unmistakably orange zest!*

1 ounce Campari

1 ounce sweet vermouth

1 ounce gin

½ slice of orange

Fill a cocktail shaker with ice. Add the Campari, sweet vermouth, and gin. Shake well. Serve in a heavy-bottomed cocktail glass filled with ice. Garnish with the orange slice.

APEROL SPRITZ

─── • SERVES 1 • ───

G: *Aperol is a bitters similar to Campari, but lighter in feel and color, due to its orange origins. This spritz gets its bubbly kick from Prosecco, making it a refreshing summer drink, and practically ubiquitous in Italy during those months.*

3 ounces Prosecco, well chilled

2 ounces Aperol

Splash of tonic water

½ slice of orange

In a tall glass filled with ice, combine the Prosecco, Aperol, and tonic.

Stir well, add the orange slice, and serve in a wine or champagne glass with a straw.

FOREPLAY

When you want a romantic cocktail that is aggressive, from its visual display to the way it hits your throat, the Foreplay is your drink. Inspired by a fiery bar cocktail we had once that included orange-infused vodka, we decided to come up with our own version. This one is Tuscany meets Baja California all the way, from the Italian use of citrusy fruit to the Mexican kick from the serrano chile. It's a fantastically sexy beverage—so colorful, silky, and spicy that you and your loved one might need to cancel those dinner reservations.

1½ ounces fresh lemon juice

1½ ounces fresh orange juice

1½ ounces Simple Syrup (recipe follows)

1½ ounces no-sugar-added or unsweetened cranberry juice

3 ounces tangerine-flavored vodka (such as Absolut Mandarin)

1 serrano chile, sliced

Sugar, for dipping and garnish

1 orange slice

In a pitcher, combine the lemon juice, orange juice, Simple Syrup, cranberry juice, and vodka.

In the bottom of a cocktail shaker, muddle 2 slices of the chile. Add the alcoholic mixture and some ice and shake.

On a small plate, pour a layer of sugar. Rub the rims of 2 cocktail glasses with the orange slice, then dip the rims into the sugar.

Pour the cocktail mixture into the glasses, and serve. Garnish with a sugar-coated chile slice.

SIMPLE SYRUP
MAKES 1⅓ CUPS

1 cup water

1 cup light brown sugar, loosely packed

In a medium saucepan, combine the water and brown sugar and bring to a boil. Stir for 1 minute, or until the sugar has dissolved. Set aside to cool. Keep refrigerated in a small pitcher or squeeze bottle.

ACKNOWLEDGMENTS

MANY THANKS TO:

Our dear friend and cowriter Robert Abele, whose friendship, laughter, and patience made writing this cookbook together a JOY! Thank you for already loving Tuscan everything and getting our true voices. Margy Rochlin, Robert Abele's other half, who has been our friend forever, introduced us to everything edible in Los Angeles, and supported every step of our careers with love and guidance.

Our photographer, Eric Wolfinger, whose raw talent, good nature, and love of food made him gifted at capturing Tuscany anywhere. Much appreciation also goes to the hardworking Allison Christiana and Nicola Parisi, who assisted Eric in the photography. Alison Attenborough and Jo Keohane for the wonderful food and prop styling. Anthony Contrino, who became one of our culinary tribe due to his fantastic talent.

Our agent, Pilar Queen, who always looks after us, and guided us through the process of creating our first cookbook!

The Cooking Channel and Food Network for giving us the fantastic opportunity to have a wonderful series to share with the world! Bruce Seidel, who sees us for who we are, and gave us a shot at turning our blog into a TV show! Janelle Fiorito, for helping us create our show, *Extra Virgin*, and for being a true visionary and dear friend. Thanks to her family and crew for their hard work! Brianna Beaudry and her crew,

for always making our food look amazing! Lee Schrager, who has supported us from day one.

Lisa Leone, best friend and Godmother to our children. We feel your love wherever we are.

Robert Poppel, who has supported us through every big event in our lives, and made so much possible because you always had our backs.

Giovanni and Michele at Bar Pitti for always giving us a warm Tuscan meal in NYC.

Katia Labeque, for introducing us.

DEBI'S PERSONAL THANKS:

My husband, Gabriele, who feeds my soul. Thank you for loving me, and for making me Tuscan. *Tu sei mio, per sempre! Non te lo dimentcare!*

My beautiful daughters, Evelina and Giulia. Thank you for choosing me to be your Mamma! Teaching you how to cook is crucial to your future, and is my retirement plan. :)

Martin Scorsese, thank you for catapulting me into Italian pop culture!

My mother, Nancy, the coolest hippie, who taught me to have a sense of adventure, to be a strong woman, and to never look back. I love you!

Stefan, don't stop baking!! We are waiting for our Christmas cookies!

My grandmother Evelyn, who my first-born is named after: you inspired me to be "old school," to feed my man, and to keep a nice home. It's working!

My Godparents, Gary and Pat Pagano, who have been by my side since I was born. I wouldn't be here if it wasn't for you. I owe you many meals and much more.

My sister, Alexandra, and brothers, Jaret and Cezanne: come and raid my fridge anytime.

My in-laws, Annalisa and Leonardo, for their direction in how to be a great Tuscan wife, and for teaching me to feed their son and grandchildren with ease and elegance.

Nonna Lola, whose stories from the "old times" have inspired me, and given me the tools to be a Florentine Queen.

Madonna, whose Calphalon spaghetti pot I "borrowed" in the late '80s and never returned—I still make all my favorite sauces in it, and think of you every time. Thanks Girlfriend! It's been a LONG road. :)

Min and Oli Sanchez for being my extended family forever.

Julian Asion, Peter Heaney, Don Marino, Paul Cilione, Claudio Camaione, Marc Balet, and Fred Brathwaite for being my older "brothers," schooling me, and having the best dinner parties!

All my other friends and family—and you know who you are—who were there for me when I needed food, a good story, or a pair of heels. I thank you.

GABRIELE'S PERSONAL THANKS:

Deborah, for being my muse and my pillar, I am forever yours . . . and will forever cook for you.

Evelina and Giulia, for your love and inquisitive palate. Thank you for making me a father.

Nonna Lola, for raising me in her kitchen and teaching me the secrets of a traditional Tuscan kitchen.

Mamma Annalisa, for feeding my stomach, heart, and soul.

Babbo Leonardo—who once put me in front of a fireplace and said, "Let's cook dinner!"

Brother Fabio, the very first person I ever cooked for.

Patrizio, Matteo, Corso, Lucia, and Marina, for their friendship that goes beyond distance and time.

Matteo and Rosanna, for always being the perfect example of what Tuscan Renaissance was, is, and always will be.

My *sorellina* Marzia, Andrea, Mattia, Valerj, Gianni, and Delia, for being my "Little Italy" while living in Los Angeles.

Marc Peel and Gino Angelini, for allowing me to practice in their restaurant kitchens and for sharing with me a few tricks of the trade.

All the wonderful musicians I had the pleasure and honor of working with through the years; you made me realize that art and inspiration are the fuel of life.

All my friends and colleagues in the Italian army, the years spent with you helped me find my better self. I praise your commitment.

All the people I have ever cooked for, please keep coming back hungry—practice makes perfect.